A MISCELLANY, ALMANACK, AND COMPANION

COMPILED, ALMANACKED
AND MISCELLANED BY

REGGIE CHAMBERLAIN-KING

BLACKSTAFF PRESS

First published in 2014
by Blackstaff Press
4D Weavers Court
Linfield Road
Belfast BT12 5GH

With the assistance of
The Arts Council of Northern Ireland

 Supported by **The National Lottery** through the Arts Council of Northern Ireland | **arts council**

Design by Lisa Dynan
Illustrations by Samara Leibner at www.samaraleibner.com,
except where indicated

Printed and bound by CPI Group UK (Ltd), Croydon CR0 4YY

A CIP catalogue record for this book is available from the British Library

ISBN 978 0 85640 921 9

www.blackstaffpress.com

For Kitty,
For Ever

CONTENTS

THE LATE READER

Chirp, chirp, chirp —
　　　What's thon? A cricket's cry!
Chirp, chirp, chirp —
　　　Somebody's goin' tae die!
O the wild wind's ragin'
　　　Ower the heathery hill;
Iv'rybody's in bed but me,
　　　The house is calm an' still.

Chirp, chirp, chirp —
　　　I hear a cricket sing.
Chirp, chirp, chirp —
　　　I wish't I cud see the Thing.
Dead long is my father,
　　　My brothers are ower the sea;
Naebody's in the house the night
　　　But mother, an' Kate, an' me.

Chirp, chirp, chirp —
　　　Kate's young — not married long;
Chirp, chirp, chirp —
　　　My mother's hale an' strong.
Then who does it cry for
　　　Wi'sich an evil glee?
Holy Mary, Mother o' God!
　　　O can it be for me?

Chirp, chirp, chirp —
　　　"Come up, Dan, tae your bed,"
Chirp, chirp, chirp —
　　　"Them book'sll turn your head."
Dan doesnae answer—
　　　She sleeps, calls him nae more;
But at the white o' dawn they find
　　　Him, huddled on the floor!

Padraic Gregory
1912

AN INTRODUCTION

The area known as Belfast first appears on record in 666 AD or thereabouts and the city has been the locus of unusual activity ever since. Not all the behaviour was devilish, not all the events were miraculous, but there is something in the crossed lines of streets and the sharp shadows of buildings that permits weird things to happen in a city – even a brick-faced puritan town like Belfast.

This miscellany of dark materials allows the reader to move in and out of the strange and shrill in Belfast over several centuries, showing how the occult, the capricious, and the uncanny met with everyday life. So too with the remarkable and the pass-remarkable. These things do not reveal 'The Other Side' of Belfast, or the 'Hidden' or 'Secret' Side. They were, in fact, all part of everyday life and the tangle of the city: the charm of superstition and the fear of magic; the discoveries of scientists and obscurities of con men; a revulsion from murder, but a love of gruesome detail. The pieces in *Weird Belfast*, side by side, will give the reader a sense of Belfast as a place of folklore, a bastion of reason, home to radical thought and primal brutality – a strange place in which strange things happen. Which is perfectly normal.

The only suitable format for such material is the miscellany, although you also might like to consider it as a companion and an almanack, with elements too of the compendium, ephemeris, digest, and collectanea. The great Charles Fort, compiler of the unusual and originator of the term Fortean, describes such data as 'the damned' and 'the excluded': that which is too marginal for science and too slight for history. He means, perhaps, those things that beg more questions than they answer. Or, if they raise no questions, they raise a solitary eyebrow.

As anomalies to the quotidian, such things do not advance a story of ourselves or of the place. If they were part of the tapestry – or even followed a thread – they would not draw the eye in the same way. Each is an independent thing, at once insignificant and interesting. They are presented here as they are, as items in a museum, a nineteenth-century French salon, or a child's scrapbook, almost touching, but not joined – brought together, because together they are at their most compelling. The miscellaneous, when assembled, becomes miscellanea and this, a miscellany. A miscellany is the cataloguing of coincidence and, coincidentally, one of the nineteenth century's most-popular was *Smith's Almanac*, written and published annually in Belfast by Joseph Smith, and deemed 'an infallible guide on all subjects treated in this wonderful repertory of heterogeneous information'.

If this current repertory of information – I am reluctant to say facts for obvious reasons – does not prove wonderful, it cannot be argued that it is anything but heterogeneous. This varied content comes from many sources: newspapers, both local and international; medical journals and academic texts; monthly magazines, including the high-minded and populist; some obscure manuscripts; some out-of-print novels; books of poetry; pamphlets; and, naturally, rumour and hearsay. Nothing here is presented from the same vantage point. What connects them only is their worthiness of inclusion: things get a little weird.

The standard for weird is moveable though and what is included here may, in cases, seem to be mere happenstance, morbidity, or local colour. By my measure, the weird embraces ghost stories and graveyards, tragic tales and comic asides, as well as ballads and broadsides, advertisements and playbills. This takes us from the supernatural at one end of a scale, via the fantastic, to the bizarre at the other: the bizarre tends to be neither super nor natural, it is most often one of Mother or Human Nature's charming mistakes. Weird is a broad church because normality, in comparison, is rather narrow. It is dependent on expectation, though, and is measured by its distance from that expectation. Thus, while a headline-grabbing murder may be notable for its extremity, a forgotten poet may stand out by his extreme banality.

Weird Belfast contains all of these things: the forgotten, the marginal, the untimely. Things that were normal then – whenever then was – seem stranger now: lectures on spiritualism; public displays of now-debunked sciences; trials for witchcraft. Equally, things that seemed outlandish once, strike us now as unworthy of comment. All the exotic spectacles and foreign nationals, the peculiar cures to common ailments, why did they once spend so much print space and drawing ink on things that we find ordinary?

A trawl through this cultural marginalia teaches us several contradictory things about the past:

a)   How things have changed;
b)   How things remain the same;
c)   That there are exceptions to both rules.

It is the last category that interests me the most.

When I used to sit on my grandfather's knee, it was not his stories of historical or political change that stayed with me, but the stories of people. Standard practice may dismiss them as anecdotes: anecdotes of characters, of sidelined events; mere recollections and vague vagaries. Even in blunt newspaper type, they are no less mystical. The formality of the setting doesn't diminish them, because the stories themselves are so small and oddly-formed that formality cannot straighten them out. Indeed, they demand that the storyteller embellish and stylise and the writers happily oblige.

It was these kinds of stories that, during hours of other unrelated research, I noted down for later. I didn't want to forget them. They were not relevant then – may never be relevant at all, in fact – but they seemed to add or accumulate into something: in this instance, one volume of what could be infinite volumes.

RCK

GILDED CAGES

CIRCUS, CINEMA, SIDESHOW, & SPECTACLE

The first theatre in Belfast was The Vaults, a murky, underground cellar in Ann Street, converted in the eighteenth century, with some industry, into a theatrical nightspot with free-for-all seating and travelling companies. The Grand Opera House, on a different hand, was built, almost out of necessity, by stranded European circus folk. Anyone who fraternises with actors knows that they are attracted to the darkness as well as the limelight. Stage, Spectacle, and Screen are naturally absurd, dangerous, and extravagant. Show is an unusual business. As is public reaction.

TO-NIGHT AT 8.

ST. GEORGE'S HALL,
BELFAST.

LAST NIGHTS.

HERR DOBLER,
WIZARD
OF THE WORLD.

Special and Last Mid-day Performance on

SATURDAY NEXT, April 7th, 1883,

At Three o'clock;

ALSO

EVERY EVENING, at Eight o'clock.

At the conclusion of each Entertainment

HERR DOBLER

Will introduce his remarkable and incomprehensible

DARK SÉANCE

Limited Number only.

VICTORIA HALL,
BELFAST.

DAY PERFORMANCE TO-DAY (Friday), at 3.

EVERY NIGHT at 8.

THE WIZARD OF THE WORLD

Two gentlemen having been selected to act as committee, the séance commenced. All light, natural and artificial, having been excluded, Herr Dobler kept his audience for two minutes in profound darkness. Upon the gas being again relighted, he was discovered securely bound to a chair with a rope – bound at the knees, bound at the ankles, and with his hands tied tightly behind him.

The committee having reported that the fastenings were of a very decided character, darkness was again resorted to. A bell and a tambourine, which until then had been quietly lying on a table upon the platform, at once began to give forth most discordant sounds, and finally took rambling excursions into mid-air, phosphorous having been placed upon them to indicate their course to the audience. The gas was lighted and Herr Dobler was seen to be firmly bound hand and foot as before.

He next borrowed a light overcoat from one of the audience and, in the darkness, slipped it on with marvellous rapidity, still remaining as tightly corded as a travelling trunk on its way to India. With the same rapidity, the coat was taken off and returned to its owner, Herr Dobler being, to all appearance, as hopelessly incapable of effort as an infant in arms. Then a lady's muff was violently taken from one of the committee and instantly found, on light being admitted, on Herr Dobler's arm. With the same rapidity, it was transferred to the other member of the committee who, on receiving it, received with it the pressure of a hand.

Nor was this all. One of the committee sat opposite Herr Dobler, with his hand on Herr Dobler's knees and their feet touching. While in this position, his whiskers were pulled and the tambourine was placed upon his head, the Wizard, as the gentleman afterwards explained, appearing all this time to be motionless. Finally, the Wizard released himself from the bonds during a few minutes of darkness, some flour with which he had previously filled his hands remaining undisturbed in the process. These feats, it should be added, were performed under circumstances which utterly excluded the idea of confederacy.

George Sexton
'Spirit-Mediums & Conjurers'
An oration delivered at the Cavendish Rooms, London
June 15th, 1873

Herr Dobler (1836–1904), real name George William Smith Buck, was a conjuror, escape-artist, and un-masker of spiritualist frauds. In 1869, he wrote the first exposé of the famous Davenport Brothers, published in Belfast by D&J Allen.

He was born in Nottinghamshire and died in Aberdeen. In between those seismic events, he toured Britain extensively, with such famed shows as the Dark Séance, Eastern Wonders, and The Enchanted Palace of Illusions, appearing in Belfast many times, where his son, George Buck Jnr, managed the Belfast Hippodrome.

A SELECTION OF THEATRES, HALLS, AND PALACES

The Grand Opera House (also known as the Palace of Varieties
from 1904–9), Glengall Street

The Ulster Hall, Bedford Street

The Royal Hippodrome, Victoria Street

The Alhambra Theatre, North Street

The Coliseum (later the Alexandra Music Hall, later the Palladium),
Grosvenor Road

The Theatre Royal, Arthur Street

The Empire Theatre of Varieties (formerly the Imperial Colosseum, Travers'
Musical Lounge, New Colosseum, and Buffalo Music Hall), Victoria Square

—— NERVE AND SKILL ——

Are required to perform this Knife and Hatchet-throwing act, to be presented this week at the Grand Opera House, Belfast, by The Sensational Carsons. This photograph was taken yesterday morning, when Miss Bolton, a member of the Opera House staff, played the part of the human target.

Northern Whig

Northern Whig
October 27th, 1936

G. L. BIRCH'S
EIGHTH ANNUAL INTERNATIONAL
CHRISTMAS CIRCUS—1947-8

P R O G R A M M E

1. OVERTURE *by Frank Rae's New Circus Orchestra*

2. PROLOGUE: *"We Proudly Present"*

3. "JIGGER" AND "JAGGER," *Liberty Horses,*
                                     presented by Gerald Portlock

4. TONI, TINA, AND TONY, *Famous Fiddling Funsters*

5. JACK MEYAND, *Amazing Juggler on the High Monocycle*
                         Direct from the Cirkus Belli, Denmark

6. LOTUS AND JOSE, *Exotic Ceylonese Roller Balancers and Jugglers*

7. GUDZOW·S ACROBATIC COLLIE DOGS, *The only Dogs in the world*
                         performing "Twist Somersaults"

8. PIERRELY, *The World's Greatest Aerial Sensation from the*
                                     Cirque Medano, Paris

9. GERALD PORTLOCK'S HIGHLY TRAINED PONIES.
      Musical Speciality by Toni, Tina, and Tony, with the Eight Ace Girls

10. TOVARICH TROUPE, *The World's Greatest Equilibrists*
                         Direct from Bertram Mills' Olympia Circus, London

11. THE COMERFORD TRIO OF IRISH DANCERS

12. LINON, *Comedy Wire Act, from the Cirque Medano, Paris*

13. GERALD PORTLOCK, *with "JASON," England's Greatest*
                                     High School Horse

General Manager	*For*	. . . .	T. B. Percy
House Manager	*G. L. Birch,* *Proprietor,*	. . . .	R. M. Drennan
Stage Direction	*Royal* *Hippodrome,*	. . . .	Victor O'Mara
Production Director	*Belfast*	. . . .	R. H. Hunter

This programme is subject to alteration

14. **BUFFALO BILL in Person,** *A Spectacular Cavalcade of Western Thrills.*
    Appeared before Royalty *

15. **PARADE OF THE TOY SOLDIERS:** *The Eight Ace Girls*

16. **"MARQUIS,"** *Hollywood's Famous Performing Chimpanzee*

17. **DANIEL, DUBSKY AND CO.,** *Europe's Greatest and Craziest Clowns*
    Direct from the Cirkus Astoria, Sweden

INTERVAL

---

18. **THE YODELLING RANGERS,** *From the wide-open spaces of far-off*
                                      Canada

19. **"ANNABELLA,"** *The Hippodrome's Crazy Comedy Horse*

20. **DANCE OF THE WILD, WILD WOMEN:** *The Eight Ace Girls*

21. **TROLLE RHODIN'S FIVE GIANT ABYSSINIAN LIONS,**
    Presented by Simon Perssons, Europe's Youngest Wild Animal Trainer
      Direct from the Cirkus Berny, Norway

22. **FINALE:** *Good-bye*

23. **GOD SAVE THE KING**

Belfast Royal Hippodrome

---

*   Buffalo Bill Cody died in 1917. He was survived by the Buffalo Bill
impersonation business, which lives to this day.

PIERRELY

In a topsy-turvy world a man who walks upside-down on the ceiling would be no novelty; but in our ordinary prosaic world a "ceiling-walker" is, to say the least of it, unusual, and Pierrely, who walks upside-down at dizzy heights, is one of the most unusual artists ever presented in a circus. His performance is indeed sensational, his act ending in a most unexpected and exciting manner. Pierrely is a Frenchman, and as a youth

Belfast Royal Hippodrome

served an apprenticeship in one of the last sailing-ships; during this time he was always in trouble with his officers, performing the craziest hair-raising stunts high up in the rigging. One day a circus proprietor saw him and induced him to leave the sea and become a performer. And here he is to amaze the people of Belfast with his crazy, hair-raising, upside-down performance. This is his first appearance in the British Islands; and he comes to us direct from the Cirque Medano, Paris.

Royal Hippodrome Circus
Souvenir Programme
1947–8

BELFAST FILM BANNED
DELAY OF BOGEY-MAN ORDER
THE MANAGER SURPRISED
TEXT OF OFFICIAL INTIMATION

The banning of the film, "Frankenstein", showing this week at the Classic Cinema, by a sub-committee of the Belfast Corporation Police Committee, announced in yesterday's Telegraph has caused a mild sensation in the city.

The film is based on the story by Mary Shelley, sister of the poet, which was written over a hundred years ago, and its theme is frankly of the "sicker" order. The producers claim to have out-Draculaed Dracula and that they produced a bogey-man film sufficient to scare the members of the committee who saw it was evident.

The history of the banning of the film began with a complaint made on the day by Rev. W. Popham B.A. (one of the joint honoraries of the Churches' Film Committee), who wrote to the Town Clerk giving the opinion that the film was questionable and asking the Police Committee to inspect it.

The Town Clerk communicated with Mr. McDermott, manager of the Classic, who arranged a private show at 11.30 a.m. on Wednesday morning.

He was quite satisfied that nothing would prove wrong with the picture. It is "just a bogey-man film calculated to thrill adult children," said Mr. McDermott to a Telegraph representative and he expressed amazement at the news that a decision was reached by a majority of three to two.

Meanwhile, the theatre opened at one o'clock and was filled with an expectant audience waiting to be "thrilled" by the spectacle of Boris Karloff (recognised as the successor to Lon Chaney) wearing forty-eight pounds weight of grotesque make-up in an effort to rouse the blasé film-goer to new sensation.

—— GIVEN FIRST "RUN" OF THE DAY ——

When the decision of the sub-committee was given to Mr. McDermott, he refused to withdraw the picture and it was given in the first "run" of the day.

During the afternoon, the following letter from Sir Robert Meyer, Town Clerk, reached Mr. McDermott:

"The Police Committee's attention having been drawn by the Belfast Film Committee to the above-named film, at present being shown at the Classic Cinema, the committee met at the cinema this morning, when you were good enough to give them a private exhibition and they came to the decision that the film must be withdrawn at the conclusion of today's matinee performance and not again shown in Belfast. This notice is to formally require you to give effect to the committee's decision which was communicated to you verbally at the time.

"I am to thank you for the courtesy you extended to the committee and the facilities which you gave them for viewing the film."

In obedience, Mr. McDermott took the film off and put on a substitute, "The Medicine Man", going on to the stage at each new run and apologising for the absence of "Frankenstein" which, he said, he had been compelled to take off. There was sympathetic applause at each announcement.

Mr. McDermott told the Telegraph representative afterwards that the patrons he had spoken to said they saw nothing wrong with the film and generally the impression was that the ban on the film was gravely unfair.

One patron said after leaving the theatre that Frankenstein would recall the giant in last year's Opera House pantomime, though he was not quite so fearsome as the wonderful figure brought into Jack and the Beanstalk by clever stagecraft. He did not, moreover, "smell the blood of an Englishman" with the same ferocity.

Meanwhile, the feature film for the remainder of the week will be "Strictly Dishonourable", a Stone Lewis picture.

Belfast Telegraph
April 21st, 1932

ON WITH THE MOTLEY
STUDENTS' DAY IN BELFAST
FRANKENSTEIN MONSTER BANNED

The Frankenstein monster came to an abrupt end yesterday afternoon at Donegall Quay. Hundreds of people witnessed its death and the only sounds of mourning came from the "Pro Tanto Quid Banned", which solemnly played the "Dead March", and the siren on the Robins, which hooted out one long lugubrious cry. Slowly the monster was raised up and down on a huge crate, then, giddy and dazed, it was hauled into the lough and without ceremony drowned.

Northern Whig
May 4th, 1932

A FINE YET MORBID FILM

One of the finest produced films since the advent of talkies was trade-shown by Messrs. Universal Films at the Royal Cinema, Arthur Square, Belfast, yesterday. It was the screen version of Bram Stoker's famous novel, "Dracula", which has also gained fame as a stage play. No fault can be found with either the acting or the production. Both of them are perfect, but the plot is one which can only result in a rather morbid film, which will only appeal to a limited type of audience. The modern film audience invariably needs much lighter entertainment. The acting honours go to Bela Lugosi, Helen Chandler, David Manners, Dwight Frye, Edward Van Sloan, and Herbert Bunston.

Northern Whig
1931

BELA LUGOSI AT THE OPERA HOUSE

The stage version of "Dracula"— that blood-curdling, spine-chilling story of bloodsuckers and vampires — which is being presented this week in the Opera House, is so well done that many people in the large audience last night must have been left pondering whether or not there are other blood-suckers in addition to income-tax collectors.

Based on the fantasy book by Bram Stoker, the play has so many thrills that it was probably in the interest of the public well-being that some elements of humour were introduced.

None other than that great Hollywood master of thrills, Bela Lugosi, plays the part of Dracula in all the horror that only a star performer of his class is capable of. The scenes are very good, particularly when he appears in a cloud of smoke to attack his victims and disappears again in similar fashion. The end comes when he is located lying in his coffin and a stake is driven through his heart.

Lugosi is ably supported by a first-class West End cast.

Irish News
July 3rd, 1951

Thousands of people all over the world have shuddered with horror at the gruesome career of Count Dracula, the vampire portrayed on the screen by Bela Lugosi. Now Dracula has come to Belfast in person and, though he is not quite so horrifying at close quarters as in the fantasy of film-land, Lugosi's performance drew at least one lusty scream from a female member of last night's audience. His own personal appearance and manner are as powerfully suggestive of evil and the supernatural as ever and the blood-curdling descriptions of his doings by other members of the cast still produce the desired effect, but the actual mechanics of the stage presentation fail to produce the eerie atmosphere necessary to bring a semblance of conviction to his amazing exploits. The strange mist in which we are told the vampire makes his appearance turns out to be very much a cloud of smoke — cleverly produced, but with very little mystic quality

— and the cries of the werewolf off-stage are obviously coming from a badly scratched record. There was, however, some effective lighting, and the excellent acting by other members of the cast, notably Arthur Hosking as the psychiatrist and Eric Lindsay as a mental patient. Bela Lugosi brought the show to a fitting conclusion with a humourous curtain speech — which had an unsettling sting in the tail!

Belfast News-Letter
July 3rd, 1951

GUN ACCIDENT

Laurence Irving, son of Henry Irving, the famous actor, has shot himself in the lungs at Belfast, but it is believed to have been the result of an accident. He lies in a critical condition.

Launceston Examiner, Tasmania
January 9th, 1892

Laurence Irving (1871–1914), actor and novelist, was the son of Henry Irving, owner of the Lyceum in London where Bram Stoker was theatre manager. The older Irving is commonly considered as the model for the character of Dracula.

The shooting took place early in Laurence Irving's first professional tour as an actor, in the Theatre Royal, Belfast. Upon hearing the news, Henry specifically requested that Dr George Stoker, Bram's brother, travel from London to tend to his son.

— ACCIDENT TO LITTLE TICH —

Little Tich (who in private life is Mr. Harry Relph) met with a serious accident at the Hippodrome, Belfast, Ireland, on August 14th. He was doing his popular parody of the serpentine dance when he abruptly stopped and limped off the stage. Thinking it was part of the turn, the audience loudly encored him until the manager explained that the comedian had dislocated his knee. Little Tich was expected not to be able to resume his performances for several weeks.

The *Advertiser*, Adelaide
September 15th, 1909

DEATH OF A SOMNAMBULIST

DEATH OF A SOMNAMBULIST

Madame Broneau, the wife of M. F. Broneau, of the Dancing Academy, Rivoli House, Belfast, during her sleep on Tuesday night walked out on the roof, fell down into the yard and was killed. It was stated at the inquest on Wednesday that the deceased lady was a somnambulist, and a verdict of accidental death was returned.

Illustrated Police News
London
February 9th, 1878

FATAL ACCIDENT TO AN ACROBAT

Hildegard Morgenrott, a pretty young music hall artist, met her death on June 21st under terribly sudden and sensational circumstances in the new Belfast Hippodrome.

Miss Morgenrott was one of the troupe of five trick cyclists. Their performance was a marvellous exhibition of skill and pluck. In fact, it bordered very closely on the sensational and dangerous. Little Miss Morgenrott, the only female member of the troupe, was undoubtedly the cleverest of a clever lot. After balancing head downwards on the head of another artiste mounted on a bicycle for some minutes, it must have been a most trying ordeal to enter the bowl-shaped construction held by means of shafts on the shoulders of her four colleagues mounted on bicycles, while cycling in a contrary direction to that which the intrepid girl followed. She had gone through the part so well that the house applauded vociferously. The applause was at its highest when the poor little artist, miscalculating her distance, came over the top and tumbled on to the stage with terrific force, head downwards, falling a distance of about twelve feet. There was momentary excitement, but the curtain was rung down with such promptitude that nothing in the nature of a general shock was experienced amongst the audience, although a few ladies fainted. It was only when Mr. Harry Downes, general manager of the theatre, came before the footlights and, in a voice deeply emotional, said "A rather serious accident having happened, the performance will not be continued." A verdict of accidental death was returned at the inquest.

Freeman's Journal, Dublin
August 1st, 1907

THE FAMOUS LESTERS
Trampoline Acrobats

These famous artistes are Danish nationals, and their home is in Copenhagen. They perform on an apparatus called a "Trampoline", which is a spring bedstead kind of affair. On this apparatus they bounce

Belfast Royal Hippodrome

and somersault like rubber balls, up and down from the trampoline to and from a spring-board-like structure fixed at one end of it. It appears easy when these experienced artistes are performing, but I can assure you it is one requiring long practice, careful training, and as near perfect timing as it is possible to get. A miscalculation in coming down would result in a broken neck. Although these artistes have performed in England, this is their first appearance in Ireland.

Royal Hippodrome Circus
Souvenir Programme
1948–9

AN ENGLISH GIANT

A young English giant has arrived in this town. Born in Warwickshire, 7 feet 3 inches high, with three rows of teeth. This phenomenon of nature has already had the honour of being inspected by great numbers of the nobility and gentry, by many of the royal society, and several ladies and gentlemen who are lovers of natural curiosities, who allow him to be of stupendous height and esteem him to be the best proportioned of his size they ever saw. He is not yet twenty-one years of age and, what is worthy of notice, he has grown above seven inches within these two years.

Look sharp or else you'll miss the opportunity of seeing the greatest natural curiosity of human nature that ever yet entertained the public. He is now to be seen at the White Heart Inn in Castle Street, Belfast, where he intends to remain for a few days, and from hence to make the best of his way to England.

White Heart Inn handbill
1840

THEATRE RIOT

At the Belfast Palace, where a rowdy crowd broke up the furniture in a demonstration over a cowboy hypnotist, some low-brows in the gallery got gay with Ada Reeve, whose sweet and dainty refinement was perhaps keyed a little too high for them. With commendable spirit, the management closed the gallery for the rest of the week and the balance of the patrons were exceedingly appreciative. "The Palace," writes a correspondent, "is a very fine hall and Belfast itself a fine town, though at times a little on the wild Irish."

Muswellbrook Chronicle, Australia
May 12th, 1906

MAXIMILLIAN'S SEA LIONS

When my personal representative saw these amazingly clever Sea Lions at the Circus Empress in Norway last summer, he was so impressed with them that he spent a week travelling with the circus trying to induce Mr.

Belfast Royal Hippodrome

Maximillian to bring them to Belfast. At last he succeeded and I am indeed proud to present them in my Ninth Xmas Circus at the Royal Hippodrome.

These Sea Lions appear to have such a tremendous sense of humour and perform their tricks with such ease, that it is difficult to believe they require three years' careful training before they are ready to make their debut in public. Mr. Maximillian has spent a life-time with these ungainly but fascinatingly attractive animals. His father trained a troupe of them which he exhibited, throughout the world, and as Maximillian travelled with his father, he may be said to have grown up with them, and learned their curious ways.

G.L. Birch, Royal Hippodrome Proprietor
Royal Hippodrome Circus Souvenir Programme
1948–9

BOXER SINGS OVER VICTIMS

Rinty Monaghan, the new world flyweight boxing champion, is an effervescent little Irishman who sings over the prostrate forms of his victims. His theme song is "When Irish Eyes Are Smiling" and he crooned it on the night of March 23rd at Belfast, after hammering Jackie Paterson into defeat in the seventh round of a fight to settle their claims to the world 112-pound title.

Singing got Rinty into the ring. He was admitted to a Belfast fight, when only a youngster, to sing and dance a jig between bouts. He's been singing more than boxing ever since. During the war, he retired from the ring for five years and entertained troops singing with E.N.S.A., a British organisation.

Many a boxer has vowed to silence the voice of the long-nosed, grinning Monaghan, but he is still taunting them with tunes. He even plans to do vaudeville shows between defences of his new world title.

Rinty is more thespian than boxer. From the moment he enters an arena, he is bowing and smiling. He dances nimbly in the ring before the bell sounds and only then does he settle down to his profession of punching.

His real name is John Joseph Monaghan, but his grandmother nicknamed him "Rinty" because, in his childhood, his favourite film hero was Rin Tin Tin, the dog. Now 28 years old, Rinty lives in a house near the Belfast docks with his wife and three young children.

He trains for every fight on Cave Hill, above Belfast, drinking goat's milk and chopping wood. His manager is Frank McAloran, former featherweight boxer. If and when Rinty ever surrenders the title to his challengers — Dado Marino, of Hawaii, and Maurice Sandeyron of France, are in the queue to fight him — it won't he because he cannot make the weight. He is a "natural" flyweight, which is rare indeed.

Townsville Daily Bulletin, Australia
April 21st, 1948

NEW CUBAN DANCE
STEPS STANDARDISED BY NORTHERN TEACHERS

The new Cuban Dance, "The Rumba", promises to be highly popular this season and to simplify the matter for the dancing public, members of the Northern Ireland Society of Dance Teachers met during the current week for the purposes of standardising the steps which comprise it. This move will prove a boon to the public. Pupils taught by different teachers who are members of the society will thus be enabled to dance "The Rumba" in complete sympathy with one another.

Northern Whig
September 26th, 1931

Belfast News-Letter
1883

Morning News
October 18th, 1886

New York Mirror
December 1886

OBITUARIES

ASHCROFT – At
Purdysburn, on 2nd inst.,
W.J. Ashcroft, for many
years proprietor of the
Alhambra Theatre of
Varieties Belfast.

Lisburn Standard
Jan 4th 1918

The Alhambra Theatre was built in 1871 as a music hall, but didn't open as planned, as some residents of the city were opposed to it and paid the manager to keep it closed.

In 1879 it was purchased by William John Ashcroft, an American singer/comedian whose parents had moved to the US from Belfast. Ashcroft was known the world over as 'The Solid Man' following his popular performance of 'Muldoon the Solid Man', a song written by Edward Harrigan about Irish-American sportsman, William Muldoon.

Ashcroft had another hit with 'McNamara's Band' which was written for him by John Stamford, stage manager of the Alhambra. The song was later popularised by Bing Crosby in 1945. W.J. Ashcroft was so well-known as to be referenced, in character, in James Joyce's *Finnegan's Wake*: 'A slickstick picnic made in Moate by Muldoons. The solid man saved by his sillied woman.'

In 1900, Ashcroft sold the theatre, having separated from his wife and suffering from poor mental health. He continued to live in Belfast, performing occasionally, amidst rumours of alcoholism, violent blackouts, and a cross-dressing scandal.

∽ MULDOON, THE SOLID MAN ∽

I am a man of great influence
And educated to a high degree
I came when small from Donegal
And me cousin Jimmy came along with me
On the city road I was situated
In a lodging house with me brother Dan
Till by perseverance I elevated
Straight to the front just like a solid man

So come with me and I will treat you dacent
I'll set you down and I will fill your can
And along the street all the friends I meet
Say 'There goes Muldoon, he's a solid man.'

At any party or at a raffle
I always go as an invited guest
As conspicuous as the great Lord Mayor, boys
I wear a nosegay upon me chest
And when called upon for to address the meeting
With no regard for clique or clan
I read the Constitution with great elocution
Because you see, I am a solid man

I control the Tombs, I control the island
My constituents they all go there
To enjoy their summer's recreation
And to take the enchanting East River air
I'm known in Harlem, I'm known in Jersey
I am welcomed hearty at every hand
And come what may on St Patrick's Day
I'll march away like a solid man

Edward Harrigan
1874

THE BELFAST MUSEUM
7 COLLEGE SQUARE NORTH,
will be open on
EASTER MONDAY
FROM NINE A.M. TILL TEN P.M.
Also on
TUESDAY,
FROM TEN A.M. TILL NINE P.M.

RECENT ADDITIONS!
SPECIAL ATTRACTIONS!

PERFECTLY PRESERVED
HUMAN HEAD
100 Years Old
WHICH WAS RECENTLY FOUND IN A BOG.
SKULL OF
CROMWELLIAN SOLDIER
FOUND IN ROYAL AVENUE

Richly Embroidered Lady's Vest of the Period of Queen Anne; Ancient Boots of Cromwellian Trooper; Old Views and Maps of Belfast; Medals struck to commemorate the Marriage of the Duke of York; Volunteer Uniforms and Badges; Pikes of United Irishmen; Iron Coffin Guard to prevent "Burking"*; Eygptian Mummies and Mummy Coffins; Irish Squirrels; Pine Martens; Birds and Fish; Gigantic Irish Elk; Great Australian Emu, & c.

ADMISSION, 2d.   CHILDREN, 1d.

---

* A term originating from the exploits of Ulstermen Burke and Hare in Edinburgh, 1828, meaning alternately to murder by smothering, to kill for the purpose of producing medical corpses for sale, or simply to cover up or obfuscate. Not to be confused with haring, to run fast.

THE NAKED TURK

THIS PICTURE SHOWS (FROM LEFT TO RIGHT)—ACHMET MUSA (THE MURDERED MAN); ZARA AGHA ("THE OLDEST MAN IN THE WORLD"), AND EDWARD CULLENS, WHO IS IN CUSTODY, AND WAS CHARGED ON WEDNESDAY WITH THE MURDER OF MUSA.

MORE RIOTS IN BRITAIN.

FROM A NORTHERNER'S NOTEBOOK

People reading the newspapers will regard the days that have just passed as a week of tragedies and sudden deaths in the North. Here is the list so far:

On Friday, the undressed body of a man was discovered near Carrickfergus. On Sunday evening, the body of a man was found in the Castlereagh Hills. On Monday, a man was found in an entry off Regent's Street, Belfast. On Tuesday, a man dropped dead at Carnmoney. On Wednesday, a man also dropped dead at work in Belfast.

In this list, I have not included deaths by accident.

Irish News
September 10th, 1931

MAN'S DEAD BODY MYSTERY
POLICE ANXIOUS TO TRACE TWO MEN SEEN IN BELFAST
CLUES IN CARRICKFERGUS AFFAIR

Though the identity of the dead body found in a field at Carrickfergus has not yet been established, members of the Belfast Criminal Investigation Department are following up clues which may lead to startling results.

The police are anxious to receive information regarding two men, one of them resembling the deceased, who was seen at the Customs House Square, Belfast, on or about the 26th August. The man who resembled the deceased was wearing a black serge suit and a soft felt hat and a double-breasted coat that appeared too small for him.

His companion is described as a dapper little man, possibly a foreigner, of smaller build, and wearing a beret.

The police who believe that the men were bound to attract attention, ask anyone who can give information concerning them, to communicate with any police barracks.

On inquiry at Carrickfergus early this morning, it was learned that the body of the man, who, it is now established, was a Jew, was still unidentified.

Irish News
September 8th, 1931

POLICE STILL BAFFLED
NO LIGHT ON CARRICK MYSTERY

A week has now elapsed since the dead body of a man was discovered in a field near Carrickfergus, and in spite of the intense activity of the police, the identity of the man still remains a mystery.

The affair is one of the most baffling mysteries that has ever been confronted by the Belfast Investigation Department.

Irish News
September 9th, 1931

CARRICK MURDER CASE ARREST
MAN DETAINED IN LONDON
BEING CONVEYED IN BELFAST TO FACE CHARGE
SENSATIONAL DISCLOSURES EXPECTED IN COURT

In a manner rivalling the best methods of detective fiction an arrest has been affected in connection with the now famous Carrickfergus mystery.

A man was detained in London on Sunday night in connection with the affair. He is being conveyed to Belfast under police escort and is expected to arrive in the city on Wednesday morning.

A sensational story will, it is believed, be revealed at the court proceedings.

Irish News
September 22nd, 1931

LATEST DEVELOPMENT IN CARRICK MURDER
VICTIM IDENTIFIED AS DOCTOR TO "OLDEST MAN ALIVE"

No information with regard to the affair is at present available from the Belfast Investigation Department, as the investigations now centre in London, but it is reported that the shot man whose naked body was found in a field at Carrickfergus on Tuesday was Ahamed Musa, a Turkish doctor.

The identification was obtained from members of a circus company in Leeds, to whom a photograph of the man taken after death was shown. They recognized it as a photograph of the doctor who had come to England in attendance on Zara Agah, a Turkish member of the circus, who is reported to be the oldest man in the world.

SCENE AT CARRICKFERGUS COURTHOUSE

Before they reached the town, the news of their coming had leaked out and an excited crowd gathered in the vicinity of the local courthouse.

Clean shaven, with his jet black hair carefully arranged, Eddie Cullens, who is 28 years of age, and is stated to be a Turk, seemed quite composed and looked with interest at the people who pressed around him.

Of only medium height, he has a good physical appearance and was dressed in a light fawn-coloured suit of plus-fours, a light grey hat, blue shirt, checked stockings, and black shoes. He carried a brown coat over his hands, which were handcuffed before him.

Irish News
September 23rd, 1931

CROWN CASE OUTLINED

Opening the case for the Crown, Mr. E.H. Mussen, Crown Solicitor, who prosecuted, said that in April last the prisoner arrived in England from America and he formed one of a party of four, three being of Turkish nationality, and the prisoner, an American.

The principal member of the party was Zara Agha, who represented himself as being 156 years of age; one was Assim Redvan; the third the deceased, Achmed Musa, and the fourth Cullens, the prisoner.

They had entered into an agreement, forming a syndicate to exploit Agha at circuses and such places as the oldest man alive, each taking a percentage of the profits. Redvan and Cullens could speak English, but Musa only knew a few words of the language.

They joined the Bertram Mills travelling circus in England: Agha and Redvan as artistes, at salaries, and the other two who were not really engaged by the management, although living at the circus, but were engaged advertising Agha and doing odd jobs.

When the circus was at Wavertree, Liverpool, Cullens suggested that he and Musa should have a tour around the country to see if they could better themselves.

Irish News
September 30th, 1931

TURK'S BODY EXHUMED AND REINTERRED

The Ministry of Home Affairs having granted the necessary Order, the body of Achmet Musa, the Turk who was recently murdered near Carrickfergus, has been exhumed from the Jewish plot at Carnmoney and reinterred in Belfast City Cemetery.

Irish News
October 31st, 1931

TRIAL OF EDDIE CULLENS OPENS

"This is a very unusual case," observed the Attorney-General, opening the Crown case. It was unusual, because neither the prisoner nor the victim, Achmet Musa, had any connection whatever with Northern Ireland, being merely here on a visit. It was remarkable for the daring and originality with which the crime had been carried out.

"It is explainable," the Attorney-General declared, "upon the basis that this man was a criminal who was actually planning to murder his companion and friend, Musa, and that he was cunning enough to try and cover up his tracks so that, in the event of a hue and cry after the murder was committed, it would be difficult, if not impossible, for the authorities to get on his track.

"You will have no doubt that this was not an ordinary murder committed in the heat of passion. It was murder that was carefully planned and planned for some time before the date it was committed.

Irish News
December 1st, 1931

CULLENS SENTENCED TO DEATH
PRISONER PROTESTS HIS INNOCENCE FROM THE DOCK

"All I can say is that, when I swore on my oath yesterday that I was not guilty, it was the Gospel truth," said Eddie Cullens in a steady voice when asked if he had anything to say before sentence of death was passed upon him after the jury at the Ulster Assizes in Armagh on Thursday found him guilty of murder.

A little pale, but calm, the prisoner stood in the dock facing the Judge as his Lordship donned the black cap and passed sentence of death. Then he turned round and was escorted from the dock.

The Judge who fixed the date of execution for Tuesday, December 29th, said, in his opinion, the verdict of the jury was "perfectly right and justified".

"It is hereby ordered and adjudged that you, Eddie Cullens, be taken from the bar of the Court at which you now stand to the prison whence you came and, on Tuesday 29th December, in the year of Our Lord 1931, you be taken to the place of execution in the prison in which you are then confined and be there hanged by the neck until you are dead and that your body be buried within the walls of the prison in which the aforesaid judgement of death shall have been executed upon you. And may the Lord Almighty have mercy on your soul."

Irish News
December 18th, 1931

CULLENS EXECUTED FOR CARRICK CASE

It is popularly held that Cullens was an American gangster. Be that as it may, his behaviour after condemnation was most exemplary.

The Jewish minister, Rabbi Shachter, who attended to the condemned man's spiritual needs, speaks very highly indeed of him.

"He went to the scaffold," said the Rabbi, "with the deep conviction that his hands were clean and clear of the blood of this man. Nevertheless, he faced death bravely, much to the amazement of those who were with him at the last moment."

The Rabbi was with Cullens practically every day for the past three months and the strain had been so great that he felt physically unfit to be with him at the last.

"Acting against medical advice, I was with him and he felt very much comforted. He performed his prayers sincerely and it was impossible to imagine how brave he was."

Irish News
January 14th, 1932

THE
MERCY
OF THE
COURT

Crime, Process, & Punishment

The Crumlin Road Gaol was opened in 1845. Its first inmates — 106 prisoners relocated from Carrickfergus Prison and forced to walk to their new home in chains — were men, women, and children, no different to the population outside the prison walls. Until 1901, those two populations mixed, as the executions were conducted in public. The free folk could see their lives reflected in the faces of the condemned, raising questions of the path not taken, of mortality, and morality. The prisoner was memento mori and object lesson. When the executions became a private matter, so too did the questions.

HYPNOTISED INTO CRIME

Archibald King, commissioning agent, was at the Belfast Assizes recently, indicted for alleged embezzlement from his employers, Messrs. Brown and Co., soap manufacturers, Manchester, a charge of conspiracy and fraud upon a large number of cross-Channel fish and provision merchants by the accused and two others having been abandoned. The accused pleaded not guilty.

Replying to the prosecuting counsel, Mr. Edward Harrison, managing director of Brown and Co., said King had been their Belfast agent since 1905.

Several local witnesses having been examined for the prosecution, the prisoner, King, who conducted his own case, startled the Court by a sensational defence. He stated he had been hypnotised by a third party who was a co-defendant in the original conspiracy charge and was, therefore, not the responsible party. King concluded an extraordinary speech by calling on the jury, like Nelson, to do their duty.

The latter, after a brief adjournment, acquitted the prisoner.

Belfast News-Letter
October 12th, 1907

SENSATIONAL ARREST IN BELFAST
A LYNX-EYED DETECTIVE

Shortly after five o'clock this evening, Detective-Constable Harkins arrested a man giving the name of Herbert Morris, residing at 38 Great Victoria Street, Belfast, on suspicion of being Ernest Jowett, who is wanted by the English police on the charge of embezzling the sum of £1,200. Jowett was a clerk in one of the banks in Halifax, Yorkshire, and a short time since disappeared, carrying with him, it is alleged, the sum stated. Harkins was induced to make the arrest owing to a description which appeared in the English "Hue and Cry".

Belfast Evening Telegraph
January 27th, 1899

POISON SMEAR ON CHOCOLATES
ANALYST'S STORY OF POWDER IN BOX
LETTER MYSTERY

A remarkable letter which accompanied a box of chocolates, said to contain poison, was read in Belfast Police Court recently, when the hearing was resumed of the case in which John Walker, his wife Agnes, and his niece Evelyn Magowan, were charged with conspiring to prevent the course of justice.

The case for the prosecution (says *the London Daily Chronicle*) was that Mrs. Walker brought a number of charges against a Mrs. Whan who was alleged to be innocent.

Mrs. Whan was acquitted of sending poisoned chocolates to Mrs. Walker, but was convicted on charges of threats and assault.

The Crown alleges that threatening letters, supposed to have been sent by Mrs. Whan to the Walkers, were really sent by the Walkers themselves, to be used in charges against Mrs. Whan.

Mr. J. Harold Totten, the city analyst, stated that he had examined a box which contained chocolates and some white powder in an envelope. The powder, he found, was salts of lemon.

A fatal dose would be about half an ounce. The packet contained about a quarter of an ounce.

All the chocolates in the box, except one, had been smeared with salts of lemon. One had been broken and salts of lemon introduced.

Mr. Totten said that, if anyone had taken one of the chocolates, he would have detected the salts of lemon at once. The work had been done very crudely, Mr. Totten added.

Mrs. Mary Walker, the sister-in-law of John Walker, said she received a parcel containing the chocolates and the white powder. Accompanying them was a letter which read:

Dear Mary, I am sending you a small box of chocolates. Don't be afraid of them. I bought them myself. They are not like the last chocolates you got. Don't be afraid to eat these ones. Hoping you are well. From your sister-in-law, Mrs. Walker, Hillsborough.

Mr. Williamson (prosecuting)— "Is that your handwriting?"— "No".

Mrs. Walker said that she and Mrs. Agnes Walker were then and still were perfectly friendly.

Mr. O'Donoghue (the magistrate)— "The alleged plot is a very subtle one. Mrs. Walker stated that Evelyn Magowan went to her and said that her Aunt Aggie had sent her over some poison. The poison, she said, was wanted to destroy a dog which had bitten the postgirl."

Mrs. Walker said she gave it some poison and the packet was later returned. Walker's dog died the same week.

Mr. W.T. Walters, solicitor for Mrs. Whan, gave evidence regarding certain letters. In cross-examination, he said he had been working on the case since 1921 and would continue doing so until his client got satisfaction.

The hearing was adjourned.

The *Advertiser*, Adelaide
April 10th, 1928

LAYING POISON

A few years ago it was illegal to lay poison in places to which domestic animals had access, but in 1927 this obligation was removed by an amendment to the Protection of Animals Act. Poison may now be placed for the purpose of destroying insects, rats, mice, or other small ground vermin, where such is found to be necessary in the interest of public health, agriculture, or the preservation of other animals, domestic or wild, or for the purpose of manuring the land, provided that all reasonable precautions are taken to prevent injury thereby to dogs, cats, fowls, or other domestic animals and wild birds.

It will be seen that any evilly-disposed person could easily find an excuse for malpractices and that may account for the many complaints about dogs having been poisoned. On the other hand, I daresay that, if some of these cases were investigated by a veterinary surgeon, it would be found that gastritis was responsible for the trouble.

Irish News
1931

ROMOR
KILLS
RATS

JUST LAY IT DOWN OVER-NIGHT & sweep up the dead rats and mice in the morning.

DRUGGED WITH A CIGAR

A strange story of how a diamond merchant was doped with a cigar was told in Belfast (Ireland), when Sydney Powell, known as "Australian Syd", was charged with having stolen diamond rings, the property of Jack Meyers.

The latter said that he met the accused and a companion in a public-house, where he was introduced to them by the title — The Diamond King. He had in his pocket some diamond rings which he had purchased in London and, when the conversation turned upon jewellery, Powell asked whether he would sell a diamond ring. The witness then produced a number of the rings.

Some drinks were taken and the witness was given a cigar, which "paralysed him", and, while he was in a stupid condition, he alleged that Powell stole the jewellery and made off. Powell was arrested in Liverpool, but the rings were not recovered.

Western Mail , Australia
November 13th, 1914

A nurse employed in the Belfast Hospital has accidentally poisoned a patient by administering carbolic acid in mistake.

Daily Mail, London
September 9th, 1888

GIRL A PRISONER
A STARTLING TALE OF AN IRISH SECT

A strange story comes from Belfast. A young Englishwoman, possessed of means, has been induced to leave her home in Suffolk and go to Belfast, where she is now not only acting as servant in the house of a member of the Cooneyite sect, but is actually to all intents and purposes a prisoner in the establishment.

A year or two ago, the new sect of the Cooneyites was started in the county of Fermanagh. Among their chief tenets of belief are baptism by immersion and a return to apostolic methods of having all things in common.

Some time ago, they conducted a mission in the county of Suffolk and among others who attended the meetings was the daughter of a well-to-do farmer, who has a considerable sum of money in her own right and has expectations of more. She became a convert to the sect and left her father's house.

The old man was almost distracted and spared no expense to discover the whereabouts of his daughter. Eventually, he traced her to Belfast and proceeded there with the object of taking her home. She had been placed in the house of a leading member of the sect in the northern district and so closely guarded was she that, at first, it was impossible for the girl's father to obtain an interview with her.

He appealed to the police and to some of the local magistrates, but, the girl being over age, they were powerless to help him in the matter. A private detective was employed, but when this man presented himself at the house, he was ordered outside by the owner. A young woman employed in one of the newspaper offices was more successful and she obtained admission to the house. What was her surprise to find the door opened by the girl herself, dressed in servant's costume! The young lady visitor entered into conversation with her and, while attempting to persuade her to return home to her parents' house, the girl expressed her willingness to do so, but stated she was in terror of the people with whom she is at present residing and dare not move, so great was the power over her. In the middle of the conversation, the tenant of the house, who had evidently had his ear to the keyhole outside, burst into the room and abruptly terminated the interview.

Lloyd's Weekly News, London
December 9th, 1906

Dear xxxxxxxx

Mr. Wilson called at my house Cliftonville, Belfast to see his daughter Ellie. Gave some very abusive language and said my brother, Wilson McClung, was going about with a woman not married to. Said he was a Mormon and a whoremonger, woman stealer and destroyer. Cooney and Irvine were worse than this. After some little time two policemen had to come and remove him off the premises.

Next day two young women called to see Miss Wilson and said Mr. Wilson told them we took his daughter away from home under age. And was having her in the capacity of a servant and allowing no one to see her and made several charges against the Testimony of dishonesty.

Following this a foul and slanderous repeat appeared in several newspapers charging a member of the Testimony living in North Belfast with having the daughter of Mr. Wilson stolen from her home etc and dressed as a house maid when the lady visitors called but would not be allowed to interview.

I gave this report to my solicitor who made the newspaper publish a full apology and admit that the report was groundless.

Robert A. McClung

Cooneyite archive
*c.*1906

BABY FARMERS IN BELFAST
A HEARTLESS SWINDLE

A sensational case of baby farming was, when the last English mail left, engaging the attention of the Belfast police authorities. Some time ago an advertisement was inserted in a number of newspapers to the effect that a lady without children desired to adopt a baby. Entire surrender was a strict stipulation and a good, comfortable home was guaranteed on payment of a premium of £15. Interested parties were requested to address communications to a house in a well-known west of England town and, in response to the advertisement, certain parties hailing from Lurgan, a market town in the vicinity of Belfast, entered into correspondence with her. An interview was arranged at the general post office in Belfast and at the prearranged time the various parties met, recognising each other by a certain signal.

The Lurgan party, it is understood, consisted of several women one of whom carried an infant. The female advertiser was fashionably attired and was attended by a smart looking male accomplice. The parties from Lurgan informed the advertiser that they could only give £10 and, after pretending to demur, the English gentleman remarked that he would have to be satisfied with that amount.

The money was accordingly handed over, but no sooner was it pocketed than the gentleman raised several fastidious queries about the child's clothing. The Lurgan women maintained that the baby was beautifully attired, but the gentleman insisted that he could not take a child whose clothes would disgrace him. Further argument was followed by a request on the part of the Lurgan girls that the money should be refunded. The request at once revealed the nature of the English couple. The Englishman remarked that he could not think of doing such a thing, adding that it would take every penny of the £10 to pay expenses. With that he and his blonde accomplice turned on their heels along the Royal-avenue and vanished.

The consternation of the girls was intense and they made appeal to a constable at headquarters and, on investigations being made by one of the detectives of the Criminal Investigation Department, it was ascertained that Belfast was merely the latest scene of a series of similar frauds which had been practiced with equal success in several cross-channel cities. The difficulty under which the police authorities are working is the failure, for palpable reasons, to institute a bona fide charge, the dupes in every case refusing to allow publicity. It is believed that several children have been handed over to the clever pair and the strictest watch will be kept by the police for their reappearance.

Auckland Star, New Zealand
June 15th, 1907

Early in August, 1895, in the city of Belfast, Ireland, a little girl named Rooney disappeared. Detectives investigated. While they were investigating, a little boy, named Webb, disappeared. Another child disappeared. Sept. 10th – disappearance of a boy, aged seven, named Watson. Two days later, a boy, named Brown, disappeared. See the *Irish News* (Belfast), Sept. 20th. In following issues of this newspaper, no more information is findable.

Lo!
Charles Fort
1931

⊖ THE STRANGER-MITE'S CLOTHES ⊖

"What are ye sewin', my love?" I said,
An' kissed her, an' stroked her dark-brown hair.
Her sweet face flushed a bright, rosy red,
An' she answered me low: "I'm sewin' wi' care,

"Each part o' these clothes so wee an' white."
Then fondled an' hugged them tae her breast.
"They're all for my own wee stranger-mite,
Who soon will come in my arms tae rest."

Och, aye! But that was two year ago.
Now, often I watch her as she stands
Ower thon oul' cupboard drawer, bent low,
A-hidin' her wet cheeks in her hands.

Padraic Gregory
(1886–1962)

FEAR BABY FARMING RACKET IN IRELAND

Police yesterday found a four-year-old who had allegedly been stolen
from her pram in Dublin when a baby. A baby farming racket is feared.

She was in a house, gaily decorated for Christmas and expensive
presents were waiting for her under a Christmas tree. Dublin news
vendors, John and Julia Browne, claimed that the girl was their
daughter, Elizabeth.

Police said Elizabeth was found in the home of Mrs. Barbara
McGeehan, 30 year old wife of a Belfast labourer. Mrs. McGeehan
has been charged with having unlawfully detained Patrick Berrigan,
aged nine months. He was taken from a pram in a Dublin street on
December 18th and found by police in Belfast.

Belfast and Dublin detectives are investigating the possibility of
a "baby farming" racket. They think that a gang, which specialises
in kidnapping and selling babies, has been in operation. Dublin
detectives are now working with Belfast police on the trail of
another missing baby. She is Pauline Ashmore, six months, who was
kidnapped outside a Dublin furniture store.

Daily Mail, London
December 26th, 1954

Belfast police are in possession of the sensational news that eight girls, all under twelve years of age, are missing since last Monday, week, from the Newtownards Road, East Belfast.

Daily Mirror, London
August 5th, 1920

INCIDENTS OF CHILD-STRIPPING IN BELFAST

SHIP STREET
NOV 1846

A notorious practice has been reported in Belfast, the much-spoken-of child-stripping. A warning has been delivered to parents, guardians, and watchful adults, as a gang is currently at large, distracting children with toys, whatnots, and doodads, before stripping the children of their clothes and sending them home without. Two little girls were taken from Ship Street and were lightened of their cloaks.

ALFRED STREET
DEC 1846

More child-stripping in Belfast, as Eliza Scott is charged with stripping a child named McMullan in May's Field, a respectable field beside St. Malachy's Church. The monstrous criminal was sentenced to two months imprisonment.

BLACKSTAFF, EAST BRIDGE STREET
DEC 1846

Child-stripping continues its nefarious rise, as The Falstaff Gang deprive another child of his finest clothes. The good, young fellow was taken from Alfred Street to a field by The Blackstaff, where he was strongly coerced into dishabille.

42 HAMILTON STREET
OCT 1857

In another incident of child-stripping, both shoes and socks were taken from a three-year-old child while the mother was distracted by tomfoolery.

Northern Whig

'Study of a Rapscallion', by Miss S.R. Praeger (Hon.), RHA, Oct. 21st 1936

155 NORTHUMBERLAND STREET
MAY 1858

Another McMullan child is stripped bare by a bad woman, only twelve years after the last incident. Jane Meneely defrocked young Hannah McMullan, of her shawl solely, on Northumberland Street and she has been charged.

∽ *ALL ROUND THE LONEY-O** ∽

There were two sisters going to school,
All round the Loney-O.
They spied a woman at the pool
Down by the greenwood side-O.
She held a baby on her knee,
All round the Loney-O.
A cruel penknife they could see,
Down by the greenwood side-O.

She held the baby to her heart,
All round the Loney-O.
She said "My Dear, we both must part"
Down by the greenwood side-O.
She held a baby to her breast,
All round the Loney-O.
She said "My Dear, we'll both find rest,
Down by the greenwood side-O."

There is a river running deep,
All round the Loney-O.
It's there both babe and mother sleep,
Down by the greenwood side-O.

Anon

---

* Referring to the Pound Loney, a small lane (loney) at the bottom of Divis Street which led to an old animal pound and the Pound Burn stream.

A STRANGE PARCEL POST DELIVERY

Shortly after nine o'clock on the morning of October 28th, a telephone message from the military barracks, Holywood, was received by Sergeant Donaghy, stating that the dead body of a child had been received there by parcels post that morning. Sergeant Donaghy, accompanied by Constable O'Neill, proceeded to the barracks where a parcel, partly open, was handed to them by Sergeant James Wilson, postal official of the KOSB* regiment, containing what appeared to be the dead body of a child. The police conveyed the parcel to the public mortuary, High Street, Holywood, and communicated with Dr. Robert Bailey, deputy coroner for the northern division of Down, who conducted an inquest in the afternoon.

Bernard Graham, postman for the Palace Military Barracks, stated that on his way to the barracks that morning he noticed that one of the parcels gave off a disagreeable odour, but at that stage he had no idea of what the parcel contained.

Lance-Corporal James Wallace, KOSB, deposed that he was the regimental postman. About eight o'clock that morning he received, amongst other letters and parcels, a large packet from Postman Graham. On taking it over he noticed the offensive smell referred to by the previous witness and together they discussed the matter and came to the conclusion that the contents of the parcel were of a suspicious nature. On examination of the postmarks, he found that the parcel had been posted in Belfast. It was addressed to a lance-corporal who was no longer in the army. He delivered the parcel to Lance-Corporal Bruce Parkinson and deputed him to give it to Sergeant James Wilson, of H Company, whose duty it was to readdress parcels received for men who had left the service or were otherwise absent from barracks.

Lance-Corporal Bruce Parkinson, KOSB, having been examined, Sergeant John Wilson stated that on examination of the parcel he found that it emitted a most offensive smell and before addressing it he deemed it advisable to examine it. He partly opened the parcel and found that it contained the dead body of a child, much decomposed.

Sergeant Donaghy was then examined, after which Dr. W.D.

---

* King's Own Scottish Borderers

Donnan stated that he had made a post-mortem examination of the body, which was that of a male child. In his opinion, death had occurred a considerable time ago, probably six weeks or thereabouts. Either the child had lived for a considerable time or was a very well-developed child at birth. There were no marks of violence on the body, but owing to its present state he was unable to say what the cause of death had been.

The jury returned the following verdict: "That a male infant child, name unknown to jurors, which was received at the Palace Military Barracks on October 28th, 1911, was dead. When, how, and where death occurred there was no evidence to show."

Otautau Standard, New Zealand
January 16th, 1912

GRUESOME DISCOVERY IN BELFAST
INFANTS' BODIES IN SUITCASE
SHOCKING FIND OF POLICE IN HOUSE IN GROSVENOR ROAD AREA

A sensational discovery was made on Monday evening by police in a house in Drew Street, off Grosvenor Road, Belfast, where, in a bedroom, the dead bodies of four newly-born infants were found in a suitcase partly concealed among some clothing. Two bodies were so badly decomposed as to consist in each case of little more than skeletons.

The suitcase with its grim contents was removed by the police to the City Morgue and inquiries which were instituted resulted in the arrest a short time later of a young married woman who had lodged in the room in which the suitcase was found.

The arrested woman, who is in delicate health, was removed in the evening to the Union Hospital, where she is at present under police guard.

Irish News
January 5th, 1932

REVELATIONS AT THE INQUEST
CORONER'S COMMENT: "SEEMS ACT OF MANIAC"

Dr. N.C. Graham, Queen's University, stated that the four bodies were those of newly-born children. He was not able to say whether these four children had breathed or not and if they had he was unable to form an opinion as to the cause of death.

From the appearance of the bodies and from the general post-mortem findings he was of the opinion that they had existed, in a dead state, for several years after birth.

Three of the bodies could not be identified as far as sex was concerned, but the fourth was definitely that of a male.

Witness stated that one of the bodies had not been in the suitcase for less than two years. The others had been there for longer periods, possibly up to four or five years.

ACCUSED WOMAN'S STORY

The accused, in the witness-box, said she was 31 years of age and was married last July. She had never had an illegitimate child at Drew Street or elsewhere and had never concealed any body in the suitcase or in any other case. She took the suitcase with her when she went to reside at Drew Street. It contained books and some clothing. Other people who lived in the house had access to the room, on which there was no lock.

When she went to reside in Baltic Street, she left some things behind at Drew Street, including books, shoes, hats, "little things", and the suitcase. She knew nothing whatever about the remains found in the case, to whom they had belonged, or who put them there.

The jury returned a verdict of guilty. The accused was put back for sentence, bail being allowed in the meantime.

Irish News
January 13th, 1932

Northern Whig

The Pillory, which will also be a part of the English village at the Scouts' Bazaar. November 5th, 1931

JENNY JO

A Street Game*

We've come to court Jenny Jo,
Jenny Jo, Jenny Jo.
We've come to court Jenny Jo,
Is she within?

Jenny Jo's washing clothes,
Washing clothes,
washing clothes.
Jenny Jo's washing clothes.
Can't see her today.

Then fare ye well ladies o,
Ladies o, ladies o.
Then fare ye well ladies
And gentlemen too.

We've come to court Jenny Jo,
Jenny Jo, Jenny Jo.
We've come to court Jenny Jo.
Is she within?

Jenny Jo's drying clothes...
starching clothes...
ironing clothes

Jenny Jo's lying dead,
Lying dead, lying dead.
Jenny Jo's lying dead.
Can't see her today.

So turn again ladies o,
Ladies o, ladies o.
So turn again ladies
And gentlemen too

What shall we dress her in,
Dress her in, dress her in?
What shall we dress her in?
Shall it be red?

Red's for the soldiers,
The soldiers, the soldiers.
Red's for the soldiers
And that will not do.

What shall we dress her in,
Dress her in, dress her in,
What shall we dress her in?
Shall it be black?
Green? Orange?

Black's for the mourners.
Green's for the croppies.
Orange is for the Orangemen
And that will not do.

White's for the dead people,
The dead people,
dead people.
White's for the dead people
And that will just do.

---

* This rhyme and other morbid games were recorded by the girls of Ballymiscaw School in Holywood, County Down, in 1906. Others included: 'Round about the punch bowl', 'Thread the long needle and sew', 'Three Lords from Spain', 'The poor woman from Sandyland' and 'Green Gravel'.

Samara Leibner

A PREVALENT OFFENCE

Two well-dressed young men named John M'Creedy and Arthur Hill were charged with indecent behaviour. Mr. Donnelly, who prosecuted, said that the offence the prisoners were charged with took the form of an indecent behaviour which was getting rather prevalent in the city. The accused were walking on the footpath of the principal thoroughfare, and assaulted respectable women by catching them and pushing up against them as if they were women of loose character. That usually took place when people were coming from church, and he was instructed to press for a heavy penalty. Evidence having been given as to the prisoners pushing up against ladies who were coming out of the Crescent Church yesterday evening, the Court fined the accused 40s and costs.

Belfast Evening Telegraph
August 19th, 1895

☙ THE BALLAD OF WILLIAM BLOAT ☙

In a mean abode on the Shankill Road
Lived a man named William Bloat;
He had a wife, the curse of his life,
Who continually got his goat.
So one day at dawn, with her nightdress on
He slit her bloody throat.

With a razor gash he settled her hash
Never was crime so slick
But the drip drip drip on the pillowslip
Of her lifeblood made him sick.
And the knee-deep gore on the bedroom floor
Grew clotted and cold and thick.

And yet he was glad he had done what he had
When she lay there stiff and still
But a sudden awe of the angry law
Struck his heart with an icy chill.
So to finish the fun so well begun
He resolved himself to kill.

He took the sheet from the wife's coul' feet
And twisted it into a rope
And he hanged himself from the pantry shelf,
'Twas an easy end, let's hope.
In the face of death with his latest breath
He solemnly cursed the Pope.

But the strangest turn to the whole concern
Is only just beginning.
He went to Hell but his wife got well
And she's still alive and sinnin',
For the razor blade was foreign made
But the sheet was Belfast linen.

Raymond Calvert
1926

—— "THAT'S A SURPRISE." ——

Henry Baird appeared in the dock charged with wife assault. When arrested, prisoner remarked, "That's a surprise." Mrs. Baird, 18 Molyneaux Street, represented that prisoner was an idle man, who was never sober when he could get a drink. He frequently threatened her life, and once drew the razor across her throat. Prisoner was ordered a month in jail in default of finding bail.

Belfast Evening Telegraph
March 24th, 1909

DOUBLE TRAGEDY
WOMAN AND YOUTH SHOT DEAD IN BELFAST
THE HUSBAND UNDER ARREST
SONS' DASH FOR ASSISTANCE

A sensational shooting tragedy occurred in Belfast late last evening, as the result of which two people are dead and one man has been arrested.

The dead persons are: Mary E. Mulholland, aged between 35 and 40 years, and John M'Millan, aged about 19, belonging to Ligoneil.

The man arrested is William Mulholland, aged about 40, a mechanic, husband of the dead woman, residing at 7 Rosebank Street, off Crumlin Road.

The tragedy occurred about 11.30 p.m. at the home of the Mulhollands. It appears that M'Millan, who was described as a member of a jazz band, was a friend of Mulholland's eldest son, a youth of about 15 or 16 years of age. He was visiting the house and Mulholland senior, it is stated, ordered him to leave the house. The son asked his chum to remain. M'Millan, however, got up and was leaving the house. As he reached the door Mulholland is alleged to have produced a revolver, a short-barrelled Webley, and fired. M'Millan was struck near the mouth, the bullet going through his head. He fell in the doorway and expired in a few minutes.

Mrs. Mulholland alarmed, ran, it is stated, out through the back door, and the husband is believed to have followed her and fired at her as she ran along a passage, running parallel to the rear of the house. She had got some distance from the house when a second shot rang out and she was hit in the back, the shot penetrating the region of the heart. She was found lying dead in the passageway.

Two sons who had been witnesses of the first tragedy ran out of the house to procure assistance and it is believed that their father fired at them as they ran up the street towards Crumlin Road, on their way to the Leopold Street Police Barracks, which is situated in the next street to Rosebank Street, as a bullet struck the wall of a building on the Crumlin Road opposite the end of Rosebank Street.

Northern Whig
April 22nd, 1931

CRUMLIN ROAD TRAGEDY
Sons' sensational story of family differences
Evidence at the inquest
Coroner returns verdict of "murder"

Sensational evidence of strained family relations culminating in a double shooting tragedy was given by two sons of William Mulholland, of Rosebank Street, Belfast, at the inquest yesterday.

"My father had not spoken to me for a long time — maybe for twelve months or more. He was always cursing my mother and she did not speak to him at all for two years."

This statement was made by Richard Mulholland, aged 16, the elder brother, at the conclusion of his narrative of events on the fatal night.

He stated that about 9.40 p.m. on Friday he was sitting in the kitchen of his home, 7 Rosebank Street, with M'Mullan, his mother, brother, and sister when his father entered and said to M'Mullan, "Didn't I tell you not to come in again?" He had previously heard his father telling M'Mullan not to come back to their house, but did not think that he meant it. M'Mullan answered "I am not going yet a minute."

His father kept walking in and out to the door until about 11.05 p.m., when he pulled a revolver out of his pocket and showing it to M'Mullan said, "There it is."

M'Mullan then said it was time for him to go, but his father told him not to go as a "peeler was coming in." M'Mullan sat down again and his father continued to walk in and out to the door.

About 11.20 p.m. M'Mullan got up and again said it was time for him to go as he had to get up the next morning. Witness went out of the kitchen with him, intending to leave him part of the way.

When in the passage leading to the kitchen with M'Mullan and his father, he heard a shot and saw M'Mullan falling. He ran out to the street, but his father followed him and when he was about two doors away he head another shot. Witness could not say whether or not the shot was fired at him, but his father was facing towards him. He ran to the barracks and informed the police.

TWO MINUTES TO GET OUT

William Mulholland, aged 13, another son of the dead woman and the accused man, corroborated the evidence of his brother in regard to the events leading up to the tragedy. When the shot was fired his father said, "Maybe that will please you."

After the first shot, he (witness) ran out into an entry at the rear and his mother followed him. He turned to the right and his mother took the left and, when he was running, he heard another shot. His father proceeded after him for a short distance with the revolver in his hand, but suddenly stopped and followed his mother.

"I have not spoken to my father only to answer him for the last three months," the witness added. "My mother told me he was not good to her and I did not like him for that reason."

Northern Whig
April 23rd, 1931

THE CAVE HILL OUTRAGE.
ARREST OF PATRICK MURPHY
BELFAST, FRIDAY

Yesterday, the police at Queenstown arrested a man who is believed to be Patrick Murphy, who is charged with the manslaughter of James Houston, Lord Donegall's gamekeeper, who was shot a week ago by a poacher. Prisoner is about thirty years of age. He was proceeding to America as a steerage passenger, under the name of Robert Johnston, by the Guion steamer Nevada, and he was so perfectly disguised that he would have escaped detection only for marks on his hands which corresponded with marks on the culprit caused by the deceased, who bit him fearfully during the struggle.

The *Witness*, Belfast
1875

—— DUTCH SUSPECT – BELFAST MURDER ——

AMSTERDAM. January 13, 1953 (Australian Associated Press)
Scotland Yard has asked the Dutch police to search for a 21-year-old Dutch seaman who they want to question on the murder of Patricia Curran (19) whose knife-wounded body was found, on November 12th, in the grounds of her father's home in Belfast.

The man is Bertold Schuitema, of Almelo, Eastern Holland, who the British authorities deported last month after he deserted from his ship. The dead girl was a daughter of the Northern Ireland High Court Judge, Mr. Justice Curran.

Cairns Post, Australia
January 13th, 1953

AN OLD HILLSBOROUGH MURDER. 1828

From the "Northern Whig" – About the year 1828 there was committed at Hillsborough a murder whose mystery was never cleared up. This was the murder of Miss Nancy Stott, a member of the Society of Friends, and her maidservant, a tragedy which has passed into the ballad poetry of the province. They lived alone in a house in Moira Street, but the old lady – she was about fifty – was in the habit of going away on her business – a curious occupation for a woman – as a leather merchant, taking her servant with her. On Monday evening 5th December, the man who usually attended to Miss Stott's cows left her house at about six o'clock. He was not to return until Wednesday. On Tuesday morning Miss Stott's window shutters and doors were observed to be closed. Her neighbours believed that she had gone to a meeting of Friends, which was holding that day in Lurgan. It was Miss Stott's custom to take her maidservant with her on all journeys. Everything appeared correct about the house, and therefore, no suspicions were entertained of anything being wrong. On Wednesday forenoon the man came, according to agreement, to look after the cows. He found the concern closed up, and the cows were lowing for food. A boy was put upon the yard wall, and he observed something resembling a bloody cap lying at the kitchen door.

An alarm was raised, and Mr. Moore, of Eglantine, with the police broke into the house, where both women were lying dead, the heads battered by some blunt weapon. In the eloquent words of the reporter of the time: "The alarm ran through Hillsborough with the speed and the effect of a terrible hurricane. The people rushed from their homes and looked at each other with a bewilderment in their gaze and a horror in their countenance which can better be conceived than described. They ran to the scene of blood, from that back to their homes, and from thence grouped themselves in the streets, not knowing what to say or do. A well-designed murder had been committed in the heart of a civilised town, in the bosom of a peaceful country, unattended by robbery, for nothing appeared disturbed in the house — silver spoons were lying about, bank-notes in a counter drawer, and the front and back doors all locked and the keys removed."

A large reward was offered, a hue-and-cry was raised, a former servant girl (who benefitted by Miss Stott's will) was arrested, but there was not a tittle of evidence against her, and the tragedy of the murder remains a mystery to this day.

There used to be recited in the country a ballad containing ten verses, by one Patrick Reynolds, of Kilwarlin, who seemed to produce a poem in celebration of everything that happened. Of course the murder was drawn in, and duly portrayed in poetic language:

"Poetic bards and sages, why silent in these ages,
To see malign outrages and base sorrocide
Strike Christiandum with terror and fill each mind with horror.
My mentals grieve with sorrow the subject to describe?
'Tis of a brutal action which some of Cain's extraction
In Hillsborough committed upon two females dear.
Who savagely were battered and barbarously slaughtered,
And hurried for to face their God without remorse or fear.
Each heart with grief was panting,
some tender Christians fainting,
The scene was so lamenting to see them in their gore;
Their clothes as if it rained with human blood were stained,
That from their wounds had teemed was frozen to the floor!
The maid was dreadful handled, was fractured, tore, and mangled;
'Twas thought she had wrangled her precious life to save,
But forced for to give over, never more to recover,
All by the deadly blows that her vile assassin gave."

Lisburn Standard
February 24th, 1919

BELFAST EXECUTIONS OF THE 20TH CENTURY

Illustrated Police News

Date	Name	Victim(s)	Hangman
11 Jan. 1901	William Woods	Bridget McGivern	Thomas Scott
19 Aug. 1909	Richard Justin	Annie Thompson	Henry Pierrepoint
17 Aug. 1922	Simon McGeown	Margaret (Maggie) Fullerton	John Ellis
8 May 1924	Michael Pratley	Nelson Leech	William Willis
8 Aug. 1928	William Smiley	Margaret Macauley, Sarah Macauley	Tom Pierrepoint
8 April 1930	Samuel Cushnan	James McCann	Tom Pierrepoint
31 July 1931	Thomas Dornan	Isabella Aitken, Margaret Aitken	Tom Pierrepoint
13 Jan. 1932	Eddie Cullens	Achmed Musa	Tom Pierrepoint
7 April 1933	Harold Courtney	Minnie Reid	Tom Pierrepoint
2 Sept. 1942	Thomas Joseph Williams	Patrick Murphy	Tom Pierrepoint
25 July 1961	Samuel McLaughlin	Nellie (Maggie) McLaughlin	Harry Allen
20 Dec. 1961	Robert McGladdery	Pearl Gamble	Harry Allen

FINDING the MUTILATED BODY N MITRE SQARE

"I HAVE ARRIVED IN YOUR CITY."
THE RIPPER IN BELFAST

BELFAST'S TURN TO BE HOAXED

The Belfast Evening Telegraph, yesterday afternoon, published the following letter which it received by that afternoon's post:

"Dear Boss, I have arrived in your city, as London is too warm for me just now, so that Belfast had better look out, for I intend to commence operations on Saturday night. I have spotted some nice fat ones who will cut up well. I am longing to begin, for I love my work.

— Yours, &c., JACK THE RIPPER."

The communication, which is written in red ink and bears several blotches, evidently made in imitation of blood, is stamped with the Belfast postmark.

Evening News, London
October 12th, 1888

AN ARREST IN BELFAST

Belfast, Thursday Night — To-night, shortly before eleven o'clock, a man giving the name of John Foster, aged about 30, and described as a gentleman of no settled place of abode, was arrested by Constable Edward Carland, at 11 Memel Street, Ballymacarrett, on suspicion of being the Whitechapel murderer. At the time of his arrest he had in his possession a bag containing a large clasp knife and three razors, one of the latter being stained with blood. He was not able to give any satisfactory account of himself, and was then taken into custody. In addition to the articles above mentioned, he had on his person the sum of £19 to 5½d, a watch and chain, and a lady's necklace. The prisoner is a man of about five feet eight inches in height, fair hair and complexion, slight build, and rather shabby dress. When arrested, he stated that he had been in Belfast since Sunday night last, and previously had been two days in Glasgow and two in Edinburgh. He declined to give any further information about himself or his movements. The arrest occasioned considerable excitement, partly owing to the fact that one of the evening papers had to-day published a letter purporting to be written by "Jack the Ripper", and threatening to "begin operations in Belfast."

Freeman's Journal, Dublin
October 12th, 1888

Illustrated Police News

THE WHITECHAPEL MURDERS
THE BELFAST ARREST

By telegraph: Belfast, Friday — At the Belfast Police Court to-day, John Foster was charged on suspicion with being concerned in the Whitechapel murders. Constable Carland deposed that, from information received, he detained the suspect in Memel Street.

Irish Times, Dublin
October 13th, 1888

THE EAST END MURDERS

At the Belfast police court, yesterday, John Foster, a man who had been arrested on suspicion of being concerned in the Whitechapel murder, was brought up.

Constable Carland deposed: "From information I received I proceeded to No 11 Memel street. The prisoner was not there when I went first. I went back about half an hour afterwards, when I found the prisoner in, and I went upstairs to the room occupied by the prisoner, and rapped at the door. The prisoner said, "Come in." I went in, and found the prisoner in bed. I asked him his name, where he had come from, and how long he had been in Belfast. He gave the name of William John Foster, and said he had no fixed address. He arrived in town on Sunday from Greenock, where he had spent two days, but he could not say where he had stopped. Previous to that he was in Glasgow for four days, and before that in Edinburgh. He did not know how long he was there, nor did he know anyone living there. I found a clasp knife (produced) in his coat, a purse containing £19 4s 5½d, and the chisel and handle (produced) were lying on a table in the bedroom. These, when separated, fitted into the bag (produced). In the bag I found three razors, a table knife, a small knife and a number of watchmaking appliances. He said that he was watchmaker, but that he did nothing at the trade, as he had an income of his own, which he got from his father, who lived in London. He said his father was a brewer, but could not give the address. I found the silver watch and chain and locket (produced) in his pockets. He said the watch was his own. It bears the monogram "A.M.R." (The watch and chain were then handed to the bench for examination.) Witness (continuing): There was a piece of broken necklet in his coat pocket. I got the keys (produced). The watch is a lever without the maker's name. I examined the clothes of the prisoner, and found he was wearing boots similar to those worn by military men. The prisoner was remanded for a week."

Daily News, London
October 13th, 1888

THE WHITECHAPEL MURDERS

The man arrested under suspicious circumstances in Belfast on Thursday night was charged at Belfast Police Court yesterday. P.C. Edward Carland, who made the arrest, said the accused would give no further account of himself than that he was the son of a London brewer, that he had an income, and that he had been in Edinburgh, Glasgow, and Greenock. The prisoner was remanded for a week. He wore a white turned-down collar marked with a small blood-stain.

Manchester Guardian
October 13th, 1888

THE MAN WITH THE KNIVES AT BELFAST

The Belfast Evening Telegraph, which received a "Jack the Ripper" letter before the arrest of the man Foster, gives this description of the prisoner as he appeared in the dock:

"He did not bear that low-class criminal appearance which might be supposed to characterise a murderer. He had quite a tradesman-like aspect. He has flaxen hair, crispy and hedgehog-like, ruddy complexion, and a short-cut sandy moustache, his hands being somewhat bronzed and not too clean. His ears project, and might be described as somewhat "cocked," while his eyes — his most characteristic trait — appear to look somewhat outwards. He has a wrinkled brow, and his head, which he slightly inclined to the right while he was standing in the dock, is remarkable for length rather than breadth or height. He was attired in a black frock coat and black vest, and his shirt, several inches of which could be seen, was of much the same colour. He wore a dickey and a large black breast tie. His white turned-down collar has apparently a spot of blood, but this might be the result of a mishap in shaving, and stress need not be laid upon it. He was not particularly anxious-looking as he leaned on the front rail of the dock with his arms folded during the progress of the trial. It may be added that the prisoner speaks with an English accent."

The Star, London
October 13th, 1888

——— IS HE THE ASSASSIN? ———
A BLOOD STAINED MAN THOUGHT TO BE THE WHITECHAPEL FIEND

Much importance is attached to the arrest, at Belfast, of a blood-stained man with a razor and knives in his possession, on suspicion of being the Whitechapel murderer. It was known beforehand that the man, who had been writing mysterious letters to editors of newspapers, was actually in Belfast. On Oct. 9th, he wrote from London to the editor of a Welsh newspaper. Two days afterward, he wrote to a Belfast editor, the envelope bearing the Belfast postmark, and was directed evidently by the same person, the handwriting being the same and the paper daubed over with red ink to imitate blood, exactly as in the specimens inspected.

Since the evidence at the inquest yesterday about the handwriting on the wall* , the identity of the murderer with the writer of these letters is generally believed.

Davenport Morning Tribune, Iowa, USA
October 14th, 1888

Belfast, Thursday – At the Belfast Police Court to-day, John Foster was charged on remand with having been connected with the Whitechapel murders. The police gave evidence to the effect that the locket and chain found in the prisoner's possession had been identified as having been stolen from a house in Bootle. The prisoner is wanted at Bootle on a charge of housebreaking. The magistrates remanded him for a week in order that further inquiries may be made regarding him.

Irish Times, Dublin
October 20th, 1888

EXCITING CHASE IN BELFAST
(FROM OUR CORRESPONDENT)

Belfast, Tuesday – To-day, shortly after 12 o'clock, a man was pursued by a crowd through Royal Avenue, and as many persons called "Jack the Ripper". The excitement became intense. The individual turned at the Free Library and ran up Little Donegall Street.

In addition to the increasing crowd, the police were now on his track as well. Scores of people from Union Street, Charles Street, Stephen Street, and Birch Street, joined in the pursuit. It was feared that the supposed "Jack" would bolt down Birch Street and escape, perchance, through some familiar and mysterious haunt. These fears were but too well-founded, though the fact that the visitor being called "Jack the Ripper" did not dispose the inhabitants to harbour him.

"Jack" gained Carrick Hill without being captured, and he

---

* The Goulston Street graffito, discovered on September 30th, 1888, believed to be in the hand of Jack the Ripper. Depending on accounts it read as either, 'The Juwes [sic] are the men that will not be blamed for nothing' or 'The Juwes [sic] are not the men who will be blamed for nothing' or 'The Juws [sic] are not the men to be blamed for nothing'.

rushed into the first door on turning the corner. Here, it seems, he frightened some children and, when the police arrived, every facility was given them to enter. Constables Britten and M'Guirk went through the premises and ultimately found the so-called "Jack" secreted in a cellar between Carrick Hill and Birch Street.

The constables placed the man under arrest and conveyed him to the police office. As he was taken down Donegall Street, the crowd was still further augmented and the cry of "Jack the Ripper" was kept up.

When taken to the police office the crowd, which were obliged to remain outside, gave vent to their feelings in frequent outbursts of cheering. It was discovered that the defendant was wearing two hats — a soft hat being inside a felt one — and carried two walking sticks. He gave his name as James Wilson and appeared to be about 43 years of age. When asked his occupation, he said "I am a comedian," which was interpreted by the sergeant in charge as meaning "a ballad singer". He stated that he had been on a tour through some of the provincial towns and had called at Lisburn and several places in County Antrim. The charge entered against him was that of "indecent behaviour", but there can be no doubt that he was arrested more for his own safety than for any breach of the peace which he had committed.

Irish Times, Dublin
November 28th, 1888

GENERAL NEWS

A man named Robert Fullerton was fined at Belfast Police Court on Tuesday for shouting in a leading thoroughfare that he was "Jack the Ripper". Another man has been arrested in the same locality for the same offence.

Macclesfield Courier and Herald
December 1st, 1888

MYSTERIOUS KENSINGTON MURDER

On November 26th, the Associated Press announced exclusively that a mysterious murder had been committed in Kensington, a western suburb of this metropolis. The body of a comely woman of the unfortunate class, about thirty years of age, was found in a frequented thoroughfare, Holland Villas Road, Kensington, with her throat cut from ear to ear. Some of the London newspapers claimed that the murder seemed to be a crime of the class committed by "Jack the Ripper". It is announced today that a young man named Reginald Saunderson, son of Mr. Llewellyn Saunderson, a prominent gentleman of the county of Dublin, has been arrested and charged with the crime.

Evening Star, London
December 4th, 1894

Illustrated Police News

THE LONDON SLEUTHS

THEY ARE WORKING HARD TO CONVICT SAUNDERSON
PROMINENT FAMILIES INVOLVED

London — The detectives of Scotland Yard are busily at work ferreting out the bottom facts in the sensational murder mystery which involves, indirectly, a number of the most aristocratic families in Great Britain, through the arrest of young Saunderson.

The young man is a nephew of the famous Colonel Edward J. Saunderson, the Orange leader, member of Parliament for North Armagh, a magistrate and a deputy lieutenant, and the son of

Llewellyn Traherne Basset Saunderson Esq., a Justice of the Peace of Dublin County, Ireland, who married Lady Rachael Mary Scott, third sister of the Earl of Clonmel, a retired lieutenant colonel of the British Army in the Ashantee war. Reginald Saunderson's family are well-known and highly respected in and about Dublin. One of Reginald Saunderson's aunts is Lady Edith Caroline Monck, wife of the Hon. Henry Power Charles Stanley Monck, eldest son of the fourth Viscount Monck. Another of his aunts is Lady Maria Henrietta Fitzclarence, whose husband is a brother of the Earl of Munster and a grandson of William IV.

The young man, it appears, is only 21 years old, tall and handsome, a most pleasant conversationalist and an expert at football, rowing and swimming. But, although so prominent in other ways, young Saunderson was far from being strong-minded. In fact, gradually, his condition of mind caused his relatives and friends so much distress that he was sent to a school for the protection and education of gentlemen of weak intellect, at Hampton Wick, near Kingston upon the Thames, England. Saunderson, according to the police, left that institute Nov. 25, saying that he intended to attend divine service at a local church.

But he was not heard of again until he appeared at the house of his relatives at Belfast, sometime after the murder.

Indiana Democrat, Pennsylvania, USA
December 6th, 1894

THE SAUNDERSON MURDER

On Sunday, November 25th, on the understanding that he was attending a local church, he [Saunderson] escaped from supervision, left Eastcote and reached London. Here he seems to have strolled about Kensington until a late hour and then met the unhappy woman, Dawes, with the result that he is now accused of her murder. The next trace which has been discovered of his movements is that he went to a school at which he was formerly a pupil, and requested a loan. He was given 26s, but on the representation that this would not be enough for his purpose more was given him. By the aid of this sum he was able to make his way to Belfast, where he presented himself at the house of a relative. Subsequently, he wrote a letter to a friend which contained a confession that he had murdered a woman at Holland Park. The matter was then placed in the hands of the police, the result being that the cherry-wood stick and the knife found at the scene of the murder have been identified by pupils of the institution. The knife was used for wood-carving, and the stick belongs to a fellow pupil. Assuming that the charge against him is well-founded it is evident that, on realising the enormity of the crime committed, he instinctively turned towards his native country, reaching Belfast by the means indicated. Thence he seems to have made his way to Belturbet, Cavan, where the warrant obtained for his arrest was executed.

West Australian, Perth
January 28th, 1895

A MADMAN'S ACT

Notices offering reward for his [Saunderson's] arrest as an insane person were immediately issued. Nothing more was heard of him at the Home until Tuesday morning, when a telegram was received from a relative in Belfast stating that "the boy" had turned up there unexpectedly and that he was being brought back to Hampton Wick in the company of his uncle. On the way home, however, he managed to escape from his uncle's care at Dublin and, for a day or so, was again lost sight of.

Three days later, however, another relative of the family living in London received a letter which the youth had written from Dublin stating that he had committed the murder in Holland Park Road on the Sunday previous, and describing, in the most graphic terms, the manner in which the terrible tragedy had taken place. This letter was at once handed over to the police and men from Scotland Yard were despatched to the Home at Hampton Wick with the knife and the walking stick, both of which, it may be remembered, were discovered near to the scene of the crime. These were at once identified beyond all question by some half-dozen people, the actual owner of the walking stick among the number.

A warrant for the arrest of Reginald Saunderson was then applied for and detectives were despatched to Dublin to put it into execution. The difficulty of finding the youth was quickly got over by the accurate descriptions of his personal appearance, which were in the possession of the police, and his arrest took place near Dublin.

The young man at the time he left Hampton Wick had no money in his possession and he must have walked all the way to Kensington, a journey which it is estimated would take him about four hours. He was at that time dressed in a new suit of dark rough Irish frieze and wore a long, dark, new Chesterfield overcoat. He had a black hard felt hat and carried in his hand the walking stick afterwards found near the body. He is described by those who knew him as a youth just over 6ft in height, and of a refined, pale, aristocratic appearance, with a curious trick of opening and closing his deep-set grey eyes when engaged in conversation. As a footballer, a swimmer, and an athlete generally he was unsurpassed by any of the other "pupils" at Hampton Wick, and was regarded as a man of enormous strength.

Tuapeka Times, New Zealand
February 13th, 1895

COMMENTS ON A MENTAL ASSESSMENT OF REGINALD SAUNDERSON

I examined him on the 24th of December 1894, and the following conversation took place (at the time of my visit, he had just had a paroxysm of excitement, in which he had nearly killed one of the inmates of his ward). He said as follows:

"I was drugged when I was brought in here, but cannot tell where I am. Everything around me appears to me as if in a dream and I have no recollection of having committed the murder of which you speak; had I done so, I cannot understand the wickedness of the act or what I should suffer in consequence. I hear, and have heard for some time, and do at the

THE WHITECHAPEL MURDER—THE CRY "JACK THE RIPPER"

Illustrated Police News

present moment hear people speaking to me, who apparently are hidden behind the walls; I have been persecuted by these voices for a long period of time, urging me to do the various acts and I believe in their reality."

He evidently was of very weak capacity and liable to do any act to which his insane mind directed him.

This case created a great deal of excitement in London, from the cruelty of the murder and circumstances surrounding it. The general opinion was that it resembled one of the series of murders committed by Jack the Ripper, the victim being a woman, whom he casually met and whom he stabbed, and hid the knife in a heap of rubbish some distance off. After the commission of the murder, he rushed off to Ireland, where he afterwards gave himself in charge. It was found that he was the actual murderer. He had suffered for some time from the hallucination of hearing voices and, in all probability, the attack was brought about by brooding over the horrors of the Whitechapel type. He was tried and his case ended in an order for detention in a criminal lunatic asylum during 'Her Majesty's pleasure'. He had sent, at the time of the murder, which was causing such sensation in London, a 'Jack the Ripper' letter to the police.

Dr L.S. Forbes Winslow
(1844-1913)

Lyttleton Stewart Forbes Winslow (1844–1913), a controversial Victorian psychiatrist, with a special interest in proving that criminality was caused by mental instability.

Disgraced in 1878, after attempting to have the popular opera singer, Georgina Weldon, committed, he turned his attention to criminal investigation.

From 1888 until his death, he became obsessed with the Ripper case, insisting that, not only had he deduced the identity of the killer, but that he could apprehend the suspect, if only Scotland Yard would loan him the use of six stout officers.

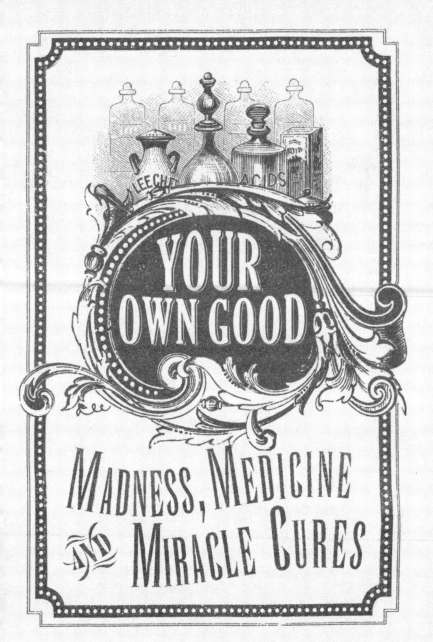

YOUR OWN GOOD

MADNESS, MEDICINE AND MIRACLE CURES

The Custom House Square was as full on a Sunday as the lunatic asylums: both were populated by those spouting madness and those claiming to cure it, oftentimes in the same breath. The medical professionals were just as grasping as the mountebanks, testing treatments and developing outlandish theories. Phrenology and mesmerism were little different to snake-oils and wonder tonics, and were just as effective.

THE MADMAN

He waited a whole year, and then set out for Saint Patrick's. A verger he enticed into a corner.

"I want to tell you something of the utmost importance," he said.

"And what is that?"

"I am a hairdresser, and I shave people in the morning," Keen Crot replied, with assurance in his voice. "There is a man who comes to me, he has come to me for the past twenty years and he, in his heart, is very wicked.

"I was shaving him one day, when he told me his secret. He told me that he had buried a beetle at the side of the Cathedral, and that it would eat away the foundations, until the spire fell down. Of course, it is a great sin. I mean I should have told you about it long ago. You will have the foundations mended, now that I have told you?"

"The matter shall receive immediate attention, sir," said the verger, with a very serious face. "You say he told you that he buried a beetle? Beetle burying's getting far too common these days ..."

"Thanks, my good man, thanks," he said. "By the way, you might mention to Lord Iveagh that the matter will be attended to. He is a clever man like myself, and perhaps he may know something about the beetle too. If he does, you can ease his mind, and tell him that the spire is quite secure. When you have finished the repairs, you should arrange to punish Mr. Garrick."

"I think that there is no need to punish him," said the verger. "If we spoil his plans for him, that should be sufficient for him."

"I don't agree with you," said Keen Crot. "But I'll call here this day month, and see what you have to say. Meanwhile, I'll keep an eye on Mr. Garrick."

A month from that date, the verger met him again.

"Well," said Keen Crot, "what did I tell you?"

"The foundations, thanks to you, are safe," said the verger. "The beetle is dead; I killed him myself in a pail of lime and water."

"That is good," said Keen Grot, who felt very important indeed. "That is good. Now what do you propose to do to Mr. Garrick?"

"It has been decided to do nothing. We think that it may be wiser to leave him alone."

" As you will. I don't agree with you," said Keen Grot. He left the verger without another word, and walked home rapidly ...

"They are satisfied to let the guilty go unpunished," remarked Keen Grot to himself, as he removed his coat in the little room at the back of the shop. "Justice is justice, however, and must be upheld; and who is to uphold it save myself?"

The following morning, Mr. Garrick entered the shop at five minutes past ten, and looked at his watch, for he felt that there was something amiss – he could not tell what. Then he remembered. Keen Crot had omitted to remark upon the weather. His smile also was absent.

"A fine day, Mr. Crot," he said.

"Fine, indeed," said the other. "Fine weather for the criminal classes!"

Mr. Garrick looked fixedly at Keen Crot as he stropped a razor. Then he sat down, and laid his head on the adjustable pad at the back of the seat.

"A fine morning, indeed, sir," said Keen Crot. He was surely smiling now. "But it remains for me to see that justice is upheld," he remarked, as he drew the glittering blade across Mr. Garrick's throat.

One of the doleful boys fainted. There was a jug of boiling water spilled by someone.

"I'll go and tell them that he's here, if they wish to see him," said Keen Crot. But a policeman had him by the arm before he reached the end of the lane, and seemed very unwilling to part with him.

"He put a beetle under the foundations of Saint Patrick's spire," the barber explained to the officer at the police station; "and as the authorities of the cathedral refused to punish him, I felt it my duty to see justice done."

"Very wise indeed, sir; very wise indeed," said a kind-looking doctor who sat beside the officer.

Unknown Immortals in the Northern City of Success
Herbert Moore Pim
1917

BELFAST DISTRICT HOSPITAL FOR THE INSANE POOR, FALLS ROAD

Established in 1829, for the relief of the insane poor, pursuant to Act of Parliament. The district comprehends the Counties of Antrim and Down, and the County of the Town of Carrickfergus. The Board of Governors meet the first Monday of every month, at one o'clock, pm. No patient can be received without a medical certificate of insanity, and an affidavit of inability to meet the expenses of a private asylum. Printed forms may be had at the Hospital, to which all communications are to be addressed (post-paid) to the resident physician.

Belfast Street Directory
1861

– RUN THROUGH THE SNOW IN NIGHT-SHIRT –

The story of an exciting chase after a delirious patient, clothed only in his night attire, through snow-covered streets in the darkness, comes from Belfast, Ireland.

Mr. Andrew Stewart, a middle-aged carrier, was lying ill with pneumonia. He was being watched by his brother-in-law, Mr. McClure, and hope of his recovery had been abandoned. In his delirium, it was clear that the invalid imagined that water was steadily and relentlessly dropping on him. Suddenly, at 5 o'clock in the morning, he sprang from his bed, dashed at Mr.McClure and gripped him by the throat. A terrible struggle ensued, but, at last, Mr. McClure freed himself and ran out of the room, locking the door behind him. Almost immediately the sound of breaking glass was heard, followed by a dull thud. Mr. McClure and his wife, on re-entering the sick-room, found that its occupant had leaped through the window, only the broken fragments of which remained. Mr. McClure at once started in pursuit of Stewart, who was clad only in his night shirt. Though his feet were bare, his footprints were clearly visible by the light of the street lamps, for snow had been falling heavily. The pursued man had covered almost a couple of miles and left Mr. McClure far in the rear, when he was observed by a postman named Sterritt, who was riding a bicycle. The wild and ghost-like figure flying along in front of him attracted his notice. Keeping the figure in sight, he blew his whistle as he rode along to attract the notice of the police, and at the Ballynafeigh Constabulary Barracks he was joined by a sergeant. Together the two succeeded in running down the unfortunate fugitive, who was quite overcome by his exertions and the severity of the weather, and was on the point of collapse. He is now on the way to recovery.

Brooklyn Daily Star, New York
January 12th, 1908

DEATH FROM WANT

On Wednesday evening last, a man, between 70 and 80 years of age, was found lying on the footpath of the Falls Road, at a place known by the name of Derry-walls (opposite the Belfast District Asylum), in a state of the greatest destitution, and almost speechless. A person of the name of Wm. Hannan, returning home after six o'clock, from work, to his place of abode, at Derry-walls, and seeing him in so helpless and miserable a condition, carried him into his house, and most humanely ministered, in every way possible, towards alleviating the dying man's pitiable and forlorn condition, who lingered on throughout that night, and until the forenoon of the following day, when death terminated his earthly sufferings.

The only information the deceased gave about himself was, that he lived at 15 Millfield; but, on inquiry being made thereat, nobody knew anything of him. Information of the circumstance was then given at the Police-office, when an investigation before Wm. Johnson, Esq and another Magistrate, was entered into on Friday, and the body ordered to be removed from Hannan's, and interred. Too much praise cannot be given to Hannan, who (in a confused dwelling and with a wife and three children) thus acted the part of the good Samaritan; and who, moreover, lost two days of his time, as a carpenter, in this melancholy affair which he and his family could but ill afford.

Belfast News-Letter
January 28th, 1840

MISCELLANEOUS NOTICES

EXTRACT FROM THE BELFAST NEWSLETTER, 19TH APRIL 1836

An interesting correspondence on the subject between Mr. Grattan and Mr. Robert Cox, Editor of the Phrenological Journal, was read by the Secretary, extracts from which we subjoin. Mr. Grattan sent the casts to Mr. Cox, merely stating that they were taken from the skulls of a husband and wife of remarkable character, who had belonged to the lower class of society, and had been uneducated and that the man was near eighty and the woman sixty at the period of their decease and he requested from him a sketch of what he would infer their characters to be from their phrenological developments.

The following is the substance of Mr. Cox's sketch:

"The man violent, passionate, cruel, and vindictive, though able to dissemble his rage; a fellow of such plausibility and hypocrisy, that, in spite of the baseness of his mind, he might long have kept up an external appearance of respectability; fond of authority, and exceedingly vain; humourous; courageous, but very prudent; not easily overreached, except by flatterers; somewhat avaricious, but so extremely fond of applause that he is likely to have spent with considerable freedom; addicted, probably, to the pleasures of the table; in fine, a man whose character might not have been conspicuous for its glaring immorality had he been well brought up; but it was to be feared that little estimable could be expected from an uneducated Irishman with such a head." This compliment to our national character seemed to be duly appreciated, if we may judge by the good-humoured burst of laughter with which it was received.

The woman: "A character the most unamiable that can be imagined; in temper similar to the man, but more reckless in her violence and fury; extremely quarrelsome, obstinate, and intractable; a tremendous scold, and one that would keep all about her in awe and obedience; her prudence and circumspection less than those of the man; extremely fond of children, but prone to treat them harshly when disobedient; very profligate, and her manners coarse, arrogant, and brutal; one whose vicinity would be a considerable misfortune to well-disposed persons."

A condensed report of the trial was next read and then the following notes of the actual character of each: "Charles Clarke, for many years, while under the influence of his brothers and sisters, an apparently respectable character. After their death, became possessed of their wealth, took to drink, and spent all he was worth in the society of a set of profligate parasites. In his later years: drunken, brutal, riotous, fearfully blasphemous, and addicted to all sorts of profligacy and vice. The woman worse than the man; noted from childhood for her coarse and violent temper and extremely profligate habits; exercised complete control over her husband; a drunken and desperate virago; fond of her children when sober; remarkable for more acuteness than her husband, but much less cautiousness; never cared what she did – whilst he, at times, displayed some remains of decency. He was remarkable for his low, coarse humour – she for nothing but her brutality; and both were held in such abhorrence as to have been totally shunned by their neighbours, nor could any person be induced even to furnish a cart to remove their bodies from the place of execution." The skulls, we understand, were lent to Mr. Grattan by Dr. Thompson, surgeon of the County Antrim Infirmary.

Phrenological Journal and Miscellany
Vol. 10, June 1836–September 1837

CASE OF JOHN LINN, A PARRICIDE

Several years ago, a cast of the head of John Linn of Belfast, who had been found guilty of parricide, was presented to the Phrenological Society

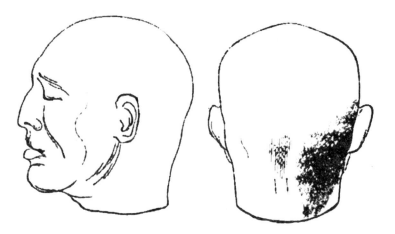

by Dr. M'Donnell of that town and, as the head is a remarkable one, we were induced to make inquiry into the history and character of the criminal. Through the kindness of an intelligent phrenologist of Belfast, Mr. John Grattan, by whom the case was carefully investigated, we are enabled to lay the following particulars before our readers.

The circumstances of the crime for which Linn was tried are thus narrated in The Belfast Commercial Chronicle of 1st September 1833:

"About one o'clock, the inhabitants near the house of William Linn, turner and wheelwright in Smithfield, were alarmed by screams and shouts from the house. John Linn, commonly known by the name of Lippy Linn, a tall powerful man, was observed with a hatchet destroying the furniture of the house, breaking the windows, crockery, &c. and two women and two boys rushed out of the house, exclaiming that John had murdered his father. The boys ran to the Court-house, where the magistrates were sitting, and a party of police was immediately desired to proceed to the spot.

"The deceased was a man universally esteemed in his station, and manifested great affection towards his wretched son, who was of very irregular habits and subject to sudden gusts of ungovernable passion. We have heard that since his committal the wretched man has evinced great contrition, and solemnly declares that, when he went to his father's, he had not the most remote intention of hurting him, far less of taking his life. When in custody and about to be removed, he asked permission to go and take leave of his father, for he had killed him.

"When informed, however, that his father was actually dead, he was seized with remorse, 'and his grief, was not merely boisterous; he absolutely roared like a bull, so that I had considerable difficulty in controlling him'.

"Dr. M'Donnell, who is the medical attendant of the lunatic asylum where Linn is at present confined, most kindly gave me such information as he possessed concerning him and also a ticket of admission to see him. From Dr. M'Donnell's account, it would appear that Linn did not manifest any extraordinary violence of temper early in life – not until he was sent to school, where, in consequence of a deformity in his lip, which had been operated on for a double hare-lip, he acquired the nickname of 'Lippy Linn', which sobriquet has been attached to him through life. Irritated by this circumstance, he used to be continually engaged in boxing matches with his schoolfellows, until he became quite expert as a pugilist, and in consequence, when more advanced in life, became an amateur, attending prize-fights, &c. and spending his money in taking lessons in the 'science'.

"He expressed great anxiety to obtain his liberty, that he might provide by his own industry for his children, instead of having them, as they are at present, in the poor-house. He was more anxious to convince that he was not insane, and had been perfectly free from anything even like temporary insanity since his admission into the asylum."

Linn's head is a large one; the breadth is extraordinary, and the whole basilar region enormously developed. The temporal muscles are larger than usual, but, after making ample allowances for this, the sizes of the subjacent organs appear inordinate. The head is of that globular kind which is so unequivocally indicative of a great development of the lateral organs. These observations will be rendered more plain by the following statements of the dimensions of the cast taken from the shaven head.

	Inches
Greatest circumference of Head	23 ¾
From Optical Spine to Individuality, over the top of the Head	14 ¼
Ear to Ear vertically over the top of the Head	14 ¾
Philoprogenitiveness to Individuality, in a straight line	8
Concentrativeness to Comparison	7 ⅛
Ear to Philoprogenitiveness	5
Individuality	5 ⅝
Benevolence	6
Veneration	6 ⅛
Destructiveness to Destructiveness	6 ¾
Secretiveness to Secretiveness	7
Cautiousness to Cautiousness	6 ½
Ideality to Ideality	5
Constructiveness to Constructiveness	6
Mastoid process to Mastoid process	6

The largest organs are Combativeness, Destructiveness, Secretiveness, Cautiousness, Amativeness, and Acquisitiveness, all of which are enormous. In thanking Mr Grattan for the valuable information which he has collected, we took occasion to send him, on 1st May 1835, the following remarks:

"It is evident that Linn was insane; but at the same time there can be no doubt that, naturally, his dispositions were quarrelsome and violent. It generally happens that the largest organs are those which fall into disease, so that the kind of insanity of each patient in an asylum may, with very few exceptions, be inferred from the form of his head. A Phrenologist, looking at the head of Linn in a madhouse, would at once anticipate violent, outrageous, and mischievous insanity."

For eight months our correspondence with Mr. Grattan ceased, but in a letter dated 3rd February 1836, he communicated the following particulars, which show in a striking manner that our confidence in the plain declarations of Phrenology had not been misplaced.

"If your account of Linn has not yet been printed, you will be pleased to hear the conclusion of his adventures. He has made his escape from the asylum under circumstances indicative of very considerable Secretiveness and has altogether evaded pursuit. It appears that, while employed in the grounds, he contrived to procure tools from some workmen engaged upon addition to the building and, one night at the end of October or beginning of November last, cut completely out of the wall the window of his cell, using his bedstead, turned upon its end, to raise him high enough to work at it. Through the opening thus made, he escaped without clothes and is supposed to have got off to America. It is also supposed that he had previously contrived to arrange with his friends to meet him."

The character of Linn is so fully discussed in the foregoing correspondence, that there is little occasion for additional remarks. Whether he was insane or not, it is clear, we think, that a man with such a head ought not to have been permitted to roam at large and endanger the safety of the public. Even though habitual conduct had been smooth and peaceable, no phrenologist could have failed to regard him with distrust and to penetrate the veil thrown sometimes by Secretiveness and Cautiousness over his real dispositions.

R.C.*

Phrenological Journal and Miscellany
Vol. 10, June 1836–September 1837

---

* Robert Cox, editor of the *Phrenological Journal*

LINN, THE BELFAST PARRICIDE

We have learned from a paragraph in a Dublin paper (Saunders's News-Letter of 3rd September 1836) that Linn reappeared there, having been brought to the head police-officer, after committing an additional murder in Liverpool.

The particulars given are the following:

"Informations were sworn before Alderman Darnley on Thursday that a most determined and desperate lunatic, named John Linn, who had escaped from confinement, was in Dublin and that his being at large would attend with considerable danger to individuals."

After mentioning the murder of his father and subsequent confinement, the paragraph proceeds to say that, after escaping, he had gone to Liverpool, whence he had returned to Ireland a few days before his apprehension. Two officers, who were sent to secure him, found him in an eating-house. When asked his name, he said it was McGouran and, after some conversation, the officers seized him. He struggled greatly, and made an attempt to take two loaded detonating pistols from the breast of his coat. He was with difficulty conveyed to the watch-house in Fleet Street and twelve watchmen could not put hand-cuffs on him. From Linn's own confession, it appeared that he had taken a place some days before in a vessel bound for America, but that it was forced to return to Liverpool, where he went on shore. Some information having been given, the police of the port went to arrest him, but he shot one of them and fled to Dublin. The magistrates of the head-office gave orders for the transmission of the prisoner to Kilmainham and the police, it is added, were obliged to get a float to convey him, for no force could have got him into a coach. Linn stated that his intention in returning to Ireland was to proceed to Belfast in order to murder his wife and children and then kill himself.

R.C.

'Short Communications'
Phrenological Journal and Miscellany
Vol. 10, June 1836–September 1837

To make a Good Water for the Face

Take two ounces of puppie seed, white, and let it ly in water three
dayes by Shifting the water 5 or 6 times a day, and sew it up in
a tiffanie or lace; then take two ounces of the best bitter almonds
you can get and bleach them in cold watter; then beat them and
the Seeds together very small, and if the Seeds be hard to beat put
in rue, then a spoonfull of plantine water to this quantitie of seeds
and almonds, and when you have beatten them as small as can be,
put all the water to them and let them stand an hour; then strain
it in a quart botle, and put to it half a quarter a pint of seek and
half an ounce of borax beatten and Searched, and half an ounce of
white Suggar candie beatten and Searched, and the whites of 2 new-
laid eggs, and Shake all these together in the glass or botle for an
hour; and keep it for your use, and if it be right it will be all of a
thickness; this water smooths and clears the face very well.

A Belfast Cookery Book of Queen Anne's Time
Mrs Margarett McBride
1711

NOTE ON AN OLD
"SURGICAL" REMEDY.

In the country districts around Belfast, and probably in other parts of Ireland, there is an old and popular method of treating a complaint occurring on the edge of eyelids popularly called "a sty" or "stilian" i.e., by puncturing or pointing at the little abscess with a thorn, yet firmly believed in by the peasantry. I have never been able to discover the origin of this method of treatment. Why the thorn should always be that of a gooseberry bush is peculiar. Sometimes one from an ordinary white thorn is used, but the former is preferred and said to be more efficacious, especially so if the "sty" be pricked through a gold ring.

Ulster Journal of Archaeology
Vol. 2, 1896

AN OVERVIEW OF DR. FREW,
QUACK & MOUNTEBANK

APRIL 1851

Dr Frew and his wife Bella Frew, were brought up on a charge of assaulting Anne Montgomery, their landlady. The prisoners were committed to the quarter sessions for trial.

JANUARY 1857

Doctor Frew was brought before the courts for being instrumental in the death of a woman named Ellen Young. It is alleged that the prisoner administered a draught, the affects of which never were that she fell asleep and never awoke. The case was postponed until after the inquest was held.

OCTOBER 1857

"Doctor" Frew was charged with being drunk and disorderly in John Street. He was fined 2s 6d and costs.

JOE MUGGINS

Joe Muggins he stood at his old donkey cart
    While a-combing his black-looking mop
When up comes his love, thon Sally Bell
      And this to her Muggins she spoke, spoke, spoke
      And this to her Muggins she spoke.

"Oh, where are you going, Joe Muggins?" she said
    "Oh, where are you going?" says she;
"It's I'm going away, love, Sally Bell
      To Smithfield to sell my donkey, donkey
      To Smithfield to sell my donkey."

"Oh, when will you back, Joe Muggins?" she said
    Or, "Ven vill you back?" say she
"At 'alf-past five, or six, at the most
      So get me a red herring for tea, tea, tea
      So get me a red herring for tea."

He had not been away scarce a couple of hours
    To Smithfield, and sold his donkey,
When the thoughts of the herring came into his head
      Saying, "I hope it's a nice one," says he, says he,
      "I hope it's a nice one," says he.

When he walked, and he walked, along Kennedy's Pad
    Till he came to that far-famed "Rose and Crown",
And there he saw his young woman lying drunk on the
    ground,
      And the people a-fighting around, round, round,
      And the people a-fighting round.

Then he sent for two boxes of Dr. Frew's pills,
    Sixty-four of big mug he run down,
Saying, "You won't get drunk in a hurry again,"
      As the pills they kept still running down, down, down,
      As the pills they kept still running down.

Then pretty Sally Bell died through taking the pills,
    And Joe he did shiver with fright,
Then he swallowed six dozen or seven at the most,
    And he kicked the bucket that night, night, night,
        And he kicked the bucket that night.

Pretty Sally Bell was buried as it might be to-day,
    Joe Muggins in less than a week;
When out of her bosom there grew a red carrot,
    And out of Joe Muggins a leek, leek, leek,
        And out of Joe Muggins a leek.

Now they grew, and they grew, to the top of the grave,
    And they were not let grow any more,
So they cut them down to season the soup
    That was given away to the poor, poor, poor,
        That was given away to the poor.

Anon.
c.1857

PITY THE LONELY

Child — It is hard enough for an adult to bear loneliness, but it is worse for a child. Nothing is more pitiful than the sight of a tiny girl or boy trying to make a real companion of a golliwog with one leg or a teddy bear without a head.

Maiden Lady — Here is one of life's real tragedies. Talk to the lonely spinsters you know, take tea with them, invite them to your parties, do everything you can to fill that tremendous gap in their lives. Their gratitude will be worth having, and you will be doing a true Christian act.

Dog — Sometimes you come across a dog who is treated with contempt by its owners because he is so familiar to them. How his pleading brown eyes ask for notice; how that uplifted paw begs to be shaken. Be kind to him, folks. Take him for a scamper. Don't "boot" him out of the way or bribe him with a carelessly flung bone.

Please help all those who are lonely to enjoy a little of the cream of life — companionship!

You often hear people say that so-an-so prefers to be left alone, but that is only because so-an-so has grown shy of his fellow-mortals, through being too long without friends.

Irish News
September 14th, 1931

KISSING AND CONTAGION

The promiscuous kissing of children is a pestilent practice. We use the word advisedly, and it is mild for the occasion. Murderous would be the proper word, did the kissers know the mischief they do. Yes, madam, murderous; and we are speaking to you. Do you remember calling on your dear friend Mrs. Brown the other day, with a strip of flannel round your neck? And when little Flora came dancing into the room, didn't you pounce upon her demonstratively, call her a precious little pet, and kiss her? Then you serenely proceeded to describe the dreadful sore throat that kept you from prayer-meeting the night before. You had no designs on the dear child's life, we know; nevertheless, you killed her — killed her as surely as if you had fed her with strychnine or arsenic! Your caresses were fatal. Two or three days after, the little pet began to complain of a sore throat, too. The symptoms grew rapidly alarming; and when the doctor came, the single word "diphtheria" sufficed to explain them all. To-day, a little mound in Greenwood is the sole memento of your visit. Taking into consideration the well-established fact that diphtheria is usually if not always communicated by the direct transplanting of the malignant vegetation which causes the disease, the fact that there can be no more certain means of bringing the contagion to its favourite soil than the act of kissing, and the further fact that the custom of kissing children on all occasions is all but universal, it is not surprising that, when the disease is once imported into a community it is very likely to become epidemic. It would be absurd to charge the spread of diphtheria entirely to the practice of child-kissing. There are other modes of propagation, though it is hard to conceive of any more directly suited to the spread of the infection or mere general in its operation. It stands to diphtheria in about the same relation that promiscuous hand-shaking formerly did to the itch. It were better to avoid the practice. The children will not suffer if they go unkissed; and their friends ought for their sake to forego the luxury for a season. A single kiss has been known to infect a family; and the most careful may be in condition to communicate the disease without knowing it. Beware, then, of playing Judas, and let the babies alone.

The *Witness*
February 12th, 1875

SUNBURNT IN A DREAM
SINGULAR RESULT OF A VIVID IMAGINATION

"As the result of a peculiarly vivid dream," he says, Mr. Charles E. Stanley, B.A., of Erin Villas, Newcastle, County Down, is suffering from the effects of what appears to be severe sunburn and he is anxious to learn if any similar case has been recorded and if any adequate scientific explanation can be put forward.

Mr. Stanley, in relating his almost weird experience, says:

"I am thirty years of age, a student and very pale-faced. Having been confined to my rooms in the city of Belfast by severe literary work for some months, I paid a flying visit to Newcastle on Monday last, when the little town was deluged with rain and the sun obscured.

"I remained indoors all the evening and retired to bed about eleven o'clock. During the night, I dreamt I was lying on the seashore in a strange locality and that the sun was shining with intense heat, so much so that I felt my face and hands actually being burned. In my dream, I remember thinking what a tanned face I would have after lying so long exposed to the glaring sun.

"The dream passed away and, in the morning, I arose and commenced to shave. What was my astonishment, on looking in the mirror, to find my face and neck literally tanned dark brown; my nose in a parboiled condition and the skin broken; my forehead covered with freckles; and my hands also tanned brown and freckled.

"The experience made me uneasy and, accordingly, I spoke to a doctor who was staying in the same house. He said I was badly sunburnt by exposure. I explained I had not been in the sun for a single hour for months and that I arrived in Newcastle in a deluge of rain, at the same time mentioning my dream.

"He was amazed and said it was the most remarkable case he ever knew, but he believed the force of imagination had in my dream affected the skin and caused the sunburn and freckles.

"The doctor asked me to write to the Press, as the case is a most remarkable one. I may add I am a total abstainer and am free from any disease or skin affection."

Daily Mail, London
September 18th, 1869

The Eugenics Education Society

President –

MAJOR LEONARD DARWIN

BELFAST BRANCH, 1911

President –

THE RIGHT REV. C.F. D'ARCY, D.D., BISHOP OF DOWN

"Eugenics is the study of agencies under social control that may improve or impair the racial qualities of future generations either physically or mentally."

The Belfast Branch of the Eugenics Education Society proposes, so far as its means allow:

1. To arrange for lectures on the facts and laws of heredity, on the circumstances attending the rise and decline of ruling races and families, on the good and bad racial effects of various laws and usages and on other kindred subjects.

2. To popularise the results of such researches as are being pursued at the Francis Galton Eugenics Laboratory of the University of London and elsewhere.

3. To ensure that the young shall be made acquainted with the principles of Eugenics, since a knowledge of them may be expected to supply an important aid towards the formation of character.

4. To intervene whenever a proposed administrative set appears likely to impair the racial qualities of the nation, and to advocate such measures as would improve those qualities.

UNCANNY GIFT
MAN'S POWER OF HYPNOTISM
EFFECT OF A SINGLE GLANCE

Here is the strange but true story of a young Irish labourer who has
a powerful hypnotic gift which enables him to soothe nerves and
relieve suffering — yet which is making life full of difficulty for him.
He is Thomas Campbell and so powerful is the influence which he
exercises that people have fallen into a trance at a single unwitting
glance from him. Fellow workmen sooner or later fall under the same
spell. Then they complain to their superiors — and Mr. Campbell is
asked to leave the job. He has held more than 30 jobs in various
parts of Britain; but his uncanny gift has eventually been discovered
and he has had to seek employment elsewhere.

Medical and scientific experts who have investigated his case
have been astonished at the potency of the influence he exerts — and
baffled in their attempts to
provide an explanation. In a
small room overlooking a busy
London street, Mr. Campbell
gave a demonstration of his
power. In full view of a number
of independent witnesses, he

sent three people – two men and a girl – into a deep trance; sewed the two arms of a hypnotised man together by plunging a heavy needle through the flesh; caused bleeding to stop and be renewed at his command.

In the first test the subject – a young man – sat down in a chair facing the hypnotist. Almost immediately, the eyes of the young man commenced to roll, then he slumped in his chair, as though in a deep sleep. At once Mr. Campbell placed his arms together and, pinching the fleshy part of the forearm, drove a needle and thread clean through. The operation was repeated until the two arms were tightly sewn together. The hypnotised subject neither moved nor flinched.

Yet the man who possesses this strange power almost wishes he had not got it. "When I lived in Belfast no one would work with me," he said. "One day a man climbing a ladder was hypnotised because I thoughtlessly glanced into his eyes from above where I was working. It took me ten minutes to get him out of the trance and all the time he was in danger of falling. Wherever I work, it is only a question of time before one of my mates goes into a trance and I am found out. Then they get frightened and that means the sack for me. I have travelled all over Britain and had more than thirty jobs."

Guardian, London
April 4th, 1936

THE GOLIGHER CIRCLE

AN EXPERIMENT IN SPIRITUALISM

ON THE THRESHOLD
OF THE UNSEEN

In the following case, I was indebted for my introduction to the sitting to Dr. Crawford – lecturer on Mechanical Engineering at the Queen's University and at the Technical College, Belfast, a trained scientific man holding the D.Sc. degree. Dr. Crawford had for some months been investigating the remarkable physical phenomena that occurred in a small family circle of highly respectable and intelligent working people in Belfast. The medium was the eldest daughter of the family, a girl, Kathleen, of some 17 years. The family had become interested in Spiritualism and had sat regularly one or two evenings a week for a year or more, to see if they could obtain any evidence of survival after bodily death. They made a sort of religious ceremony of their sittings, always opening with prayer and hymns, and when at last phenomena came, their unseen visitors were greeted with delight and respect. Obviously they were uncritical, simple, honest, kind-hearted people; Dr. Crawford having assured himself they had no pecuniary or other motive, such as notoriety, to gain, was allowed and indeed welcomed to make a searching and critical investigation. This he did, devising elaborate and ingenious apparatus to test the phenomena, which he is describing in a work he is about to publish. *Inter alia* he found that the weight of the medium increased as the amount of the weight of the table or other object which was levitated had decreased.

W.J. Crawford, 1921

I was permitted to have an evening sitting with the family, Dr. Crawford accompanying me. We sat outside the small family circle; the room was illuminated with a bright gas flame burning in a lantern, with a large red glass window, on the mantelpiece. The room was small and, as our eyes got accustomed to the light, we could see all the sitters clearly. They sat round a small table with hands joined together, but no one touching the table. Very soon knocks came and messages were spelt out as one of us repeated the alphabet aloud. Suddenly the knocks increased in violence and, being encouraged, a tremendous bang came which shook the room and resembled the blow of a sledge hammer on an anvil. A tin trumpet which had been placed below the table now poked out its smaller end close under the top of the table near where I was sitting. I was allowed to try and catch it, but it dodged all my attempts in the most amusing way. The medium on the opposite side sat perfectly still, while, at my request, all held up their joined hands so that I could see no one was touching the trumpet, as it played peep-bo with me. Sounds like the sawing of wood, the bouncing of a ball, and other noises occurred, which were inexplicable.

Then the table began to rise from the floor some 18 inches and remained so suspended and quite level. I was allowed to go up to the table and saw clearly no one was touching it, a clear space separating the sitters from the table. I tried to press the table down and, though I exerted all my strength, could not do so; then I climbed up on the table and sat on it, my feet off the floor, when I was swayed to and fro and finally tipped off. The table of its own accord now turned upside down, no one touching it, and I tried to lift it off the ground, but it could not be stirred, it appeared screwed down to the floor. At my request, all the sitters' clasped hands had been kept raised above their heads and I could see that no one was touching the table; —when I desisted from trying to lift the inverted table from the floor, it righted itself again of its own accord, no one helping it. Numerous sounds displaying an amused intelligence then came and, after each individual present had been greeted with some farewell raps, the sitting ended.

It is difficult to imagine how the cleverest conjurer with elaborate apparatus could have performed what I have described; here were a simple family group of earnest seekers, on whose privacy I had intruded and who had suffered Dr. Crawford for 6 months or more to put them to the greatest inconvenience without any remuneration whatever.

William Barrett
1918

THE VITAL MESSAGE

A friend, in whose judgment and veracity I have absolute confidence, was present at one of Dr. Crawford's experiments with Kathleen Goligher, who is, it may be remarked, an unpaid medium. My friend touched the column of force and found it could be felt by the hand though invisible to the eye. It is clear that we are in touch with some entirely new form both of matter and of energy.

Sir Arthur Conan Doyle
1919

ONE HUNDRED CASES OF SURVIVAL AFTER DEATH

Dr. W. J. Crawford of the Technical Institute, Belfast, experimenting with a non-professional medium, Miss Kathleen Goligher (now Lady G. Donaldson), saw table movements without contacts of any kind.

He drew the inference that the ectoplasm, issuing from the medium, materialized itself into rigid rods, and by this means objects were psychically raised. "The cantilever method is made use of for light bodies or when the applied forces are small, and the strut method for heavy bodies or when the applied forces are large."

At this stage the reader may well say, "These scientific tests on the movement of objects without applied normal force are very interesting and, as Dr. Crawford claimed, he may have had such demonstrated again and again under test conditions to his satisfaction, but what connection have these tests with the question of survival? Undoubtedly, it is very interesting to see a chair apparently of its own accord rise into the air, but how does that prove that the personality of man has survived bodily death?"

A.T. Baird
1944

NOTE ON THE USE OF CARMINE IN TRACING THE PATHS OF THE PLASMA TO AND FROM THE MEDIUM'S BODY

I wish to draw the attention of those engaged in psychic investigation to a method of research which I have found useful. I may call it the 'staining' method. It consists in the use of various coloured materials in the form of powder. The material I have found most useful is powdered carmine.

Whenever phenomena of the physical order occur, this method can be employed with advantage. In all such phenomena, a substance which we may call 'plasma' issues from the body of the medium. The quantity may be large, as in materialisation phenomena, or small, as in telekinetic phenomena, but whether large or small, my experiments show that there is always some of it present. Of course, plasma is not the only component (so to speak) of a psychic instrument, but it is that part of the structure which has obviously material form.

A problem such as the following might arise: From what part of the medium's body does the plasma issue, and does it return by the same or another route?

W.J. Crawford
Light
March 6th, 1920

Sir. Arthur tells me he thinks that the power comes from the womb, it certainly is a wonderful affair and there is no telling how far all this may lead.

Harry Houdini

Personal letter to W.J. Crawford
June 24th, 1920

THE PSYCHIC STRUCTURES AT THE GOLIGHER CIRCLE

In many of the experiments already described, as well as a well-defined carmine path from the feet, there were visible distinct traces of carmine up the stockings as far as the knees and even up to the top of the stockings. Usually, these carmine paths were thickest and most plainly visible round about the ball of the calves at the back and, usually, there was more carmine on the stockings between the legs than on the outside. The question then arose as to whether there was a flow of plasma from the medium's body down the legs, as well as the flow from the feet upwards or, indeed, whether the whole of the plasma did not come from the trunk of the medium, flow down the legs and then, in some peculiar manner and for some particular reason, connect with the building up of the psychic structures, enter her shoes and fill up the space between stocking and leather. For, after all, it has to be remembered that our feet and legs are only pieces of apparatus to enable us to move about, analogous to the wheels of a cart, and that the great centres of nervous energy and reproductive activity are within the body proper.

W.J. Crawford
1921

A MAGICIAN AMONG THE SPIRITS

While at Mr. Fielding's home in London I had the pleasure of meeting this Dr. Crawford and talking with him for several hours. During the talk he showed me pictures of what he claimed was ectoplasm exuding from different parts of Kathleen Goligher's body and told me he was going to use them in a forthcoming book.

"Do you honestly believe that everything you have experienced through your contact and experiments with the girl is absolutely genuine?" I asked him.

"I am positive in my belief," he answered.

Harry Houdini
1924

WHAT IS YOUR OPINION OF THE QUESTION OF CONSCIOUS OR UNCONSCIOUS FRAUD AT SÉANCES FOR PHYSICAL PHENOMENA?

While recognising that both varieties of fraud exist, I am confident that they have been much overrated. Even at séances, such as the Golighers', where everything is above suspicion, where all phenomena can be demonstrated with the greatest ease to be genuine to the last detail, things happen which to a superficial observer might appear fraudulent.

Thus things happen in the séance-room which, from the very nature of the case, sometimes bear a superficial appearance of fraud, though in a properly conducted circle it is only superficial, and the true and genuine nature of the phenomena can always be discovered by a little investigation. I am, therefore, wary of accepting off-hand any fraud hypothesis.

Experiments in Psychical Science
W.J. Crawford
1919

THE NEW SPIRITUALISM

As for Dr. Crawford's "Reality of Psychic Phenomena", the details of his experiments with the medium Kathleen Goligher, who, by what he calls a "psychic cantilever" can exude matter weighing as much as 54 1/2 pounds from her body (to which it ultimately returns), show that chances of deception are not excluded. His book gives a photograph of the medium, but unsatisfactorily omits the photograph of the smear of the cantilever, which, he says, is to be noticed on the negative. Will he not bring the medium and the weighing machine and the table to London and submit the experiment to a company of scientists and conjurors, who shall be satisfied that every possible element of fraud is eliminated and no qualifying conditions imposed?

New York Times
1919

STUDY OF THE WORKING END OF THE PSYCHIC STRUCTURE BY MEANS OF IMPRESSIONS MADE BY IT ON CLAY OR PUTTY

If a tin or box containing modeller's clay, or putty, be placed within the circle space the operators can, on request, make various marks on the clay, which marks are permanent and afford an indication of the shape and characteristics of the rod end which produces them.

As the floor of some of the impressions seemed to be sometimes lined with marks which resembled stocking marks, and as others of the impressions were more or less like boot marks or shoe marks, and accordingly, there was the question to outsiders of conscious or unconscious fraud on the part of the medium or members of the circle, we decided that while investigating this

W.J. Crawford, 1921

matter the sitters should have their feet and legs so tied that no one could get within 18 in. of the clay while the impressions were being obtained.

It is to be remembered that the medium and members of the circle were just as interested as I was, and that they readily assented to anything I proposed in order to render the results as certain as possible and beyond any reasonable suspicion of doubt. Accordingly, when the medium had seated herself on her chair, I tied her ankles together very tightly with fine strong whipcord, using two or three separate pieces of cord; then I tied her ankles to the back bar under her chair. The consequence was that the medium could not get within 18 inches of the front of the vessel containing the clay.

First Generalisation: When the medium wears stockings nearly every psychic impression is lined with stocking marks.

Experiments in Psychical Science
W.J. Crawford
1919

Occultism

At the séances in Belfast, which, like all kindred gatherings, are opened and closed with hymns and prayers, lulling the company into Dreamland, the medium, Miss Kathleen Goligher, sits on a chair placed on a weighing machine. The "intelligent control", as the spirit assumed to be present is named, is asked to take out matter from the medium's body to be used as a cantilever whereby she can lift a table within reach weighing about ten pounds (the maximum weight of another table is sixteen), with which, apparently, she is not in contact. The control gives raps, and the weight of the medium lessens in proportion to their number, sometimes decreasing nearly half a hundredweight. Ultimately, these spiritual cantilevers or psychic rapping rods, as they are named, return to the body of the medium. During the performance, the room, under the usual conditions, is dimly lighted; no one is allowed to pass between the medium and the table, because it is said that serious bodily harm would thereby occur to her. Doubtless, a damaged reputation might also result.

Mr. William Marriott, the most experienced exposer of mediums in this country, told Dr. Ivor Tuckett that he could make his weight increase and decrease, and a table rise in the air, under conditions identical with those of the Goligher circle.

Edward Clodd
Lectures delivered in the Royal Institution
May 17th & 24th, 1921

THE WORK OF DR. W. J. CRAWFORD

As the records contained in Dr Crawford's first book, *The Reality of Psychic Phenomena*, made their first appearance in *Light*, which led to my personal acquaintance with the author, who, just prior to his tragic death, desired that I should assist in preparing the present work for the Press, I may perhaps be allowed a few prefatory words. In his last letter to me (received after his untimely death) he explained that his collapse was due entirely to overwork, and he wrote:

W.J. Crawford, 1918

"My psychic work was all done before the collapse, and is the most perfect work I have done in my life. Everything connected with it is absolutely correct, and will bear every scrutiny. It was done when my brain was working perfectly, and it could not be responsible for what has occurred."

And in another part of his letter he said:

"I wish to reaffirm my belief that the grave does not finish all."

These two extracts from a long and affecting letter may be appropriately quoted here. For the rest, I may pay a tribute to the careful, courageous, and most valuable work of the departed scientist, in an obscure but tremendously important branch of scientific research. I could say much about the present book, with its remarkable elucidation of many problems connected with the physical phenomena of spiritualism, but I content myself with a reference to such experiments as those with the soft clay and the methylene blue, which finally clear away certain suspicions that have always attached to physical mediums in connection with materialisation phenomena, amongst uninstructed investigators. This is not the least valuable part of a valuable book.

David Gow, Editor of "Light"

October 25th, 1920

Preface to *The Psychic Structures at the Goligher Circle*
W.J. Crawford
1920

INQUISITION ON THE DEATH OF DR. W.J. CRAWFORD

THE DEPOSITION OF ELIZABETH CRAWFORD

...who, being duly sworn upon her oath saith: I live at Brook Terrace, Park Avenue, Sydenham. The body the jury has viewed is that of my husband William Jackson Crawford, he was 40 years of age. He was a teacher. I last saw him alive yesterday at 10.20am. He was then in his usual health. He has been sleepless for 4 weeks past. I had a line sent by him from Clandeboye about 2pm yesterday saying he was going for a motor drive.

THE DEPOSITION OF SERGEANT MATTHEW MC-

I am stationed in Bangor. At 8.30am today, I received a phone message that there was the dead body of a man lying on the rocks at the Girls Home, Bangor. Deceased was lying dead on the rocks, dressed except that his overcoat was off, lying a few yards from him. I searched him and found the following property: a sealed packet addressed to his wife; a letter also addressed to his wife; a silver watch stopped at 7.50, also a gold chain; a bunch of keys and a purse with 15/6 silver and sevenpence in coppers; a cheque book; a noggin bottle 3/4 full of whiskey; a pipe and tobacco pouch; a packet labelled "carmine"; also 2 matchboxes; a pen knife; and a small address book.

THE DEPOSITION OF DR. J.M. MITCHELL

I am medical officer of Bangor Dispensary district. I have made an external examination of the body of deceased. There are not any marks of violence. There was some froth coming from his mouth. His face is very flushed. In my opinion, the cause of his death was poisoning, probably by cyanide of potassium.

July 31st, 1920

THE GOLIGHER CIRCLE, MAY TO AUGUST 1921

By careful measurements, I had found that all the results of sitting No. 10 could be produced by the medium leaning forward out of her chair, supporting herself with one foot on the floor and using the other foot for producing 'phenomena.' As this involved no lowering of the head, the 'locator' would not have indicated any displacement.

E.E. Fournier d'Albe
1922

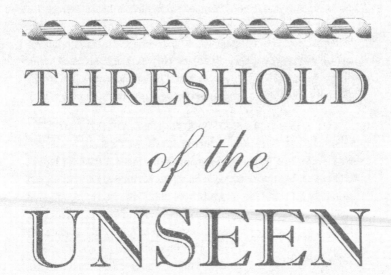

THRESHOLD
of the
UNSEEN

The UNNATURAL
in FOLK *and* SCIENCE

Dr W.J. Crawford's experiments with the psychics of the Goligher family are part of a fine tradition in which science and folklore come together, finding common ground in their need to interpret behaviour and analyse effects. They seek to provide an explanation where there is none: a theory of fairies, a theory of ghosts. Any explanation is better than none, although some are more rigorous than others.

Belfast was a late-blooming city, flowering in the Age of Science. People were lured there from the country, attracted by chance and advancement, but bringing with them their own superstitions and ways. In Belfast, science and folklore clashed and cohered, for they were asking the same questions: Why does this happen? How does this happen? And what will happen to us all?

RAINING FISH

Not long ago it rained more than water near Belfast. It rained fishes! During a thunderstorm, dozens of small red-brown fish about two inches long fell on the roof of a bungalow. The nearest important piece of water is Strangford Lough, two miles distant, and there is no river in the neighbourhood.

A professor of Queen's University, Belfast, states that as far as he knows this is Ireland's first fish shower, but it is not the first that has occurred in Great Britain.

In the past, people have attributed these showers to witchcraft, but the truth is, of course, that the wind was at the bottom of the mischief. Travelling with a circular motion, the wind will sweep up light objects like a gigantic vacuum cleaner and bear them for miles through the air.

In every case recorded these strange showers have been accompanied by extraordinary weather; waterspouts, whirlwinds, or tremendous thunderstorms. Whole hedges were blackened in the Irish storm.

Evening Post, London
November 6th, 1931

—— KUDA BUX, FROM KASHMIR ——

The man with the x-ray eyes, who is appearing at the Grand Opera House, Belfast, this week, undergoing one of the tests applied to him on the stage yesterday morning. A panel of doctors and Pressmen were present, who put him through several exhaustive tests, which he passed quite easily. The writing on the blackboard in the picture is in Hindustani and Hebrew, of which Kuda Bux re-wrote every word securely blindfolded.

Northern Whig
October 23rd, 1937

THE FAIRY THORN

"Get up, our Anna dear, from the weary spinning-wheel;
For your father's on the hill, and your mother is asleep;
Come up above the crags, and we'll dance a Highland reel
    Around the Fairy Thorn on the steep."

At Anna Grace's door 'twas thus the maidens cried,
Three merry maidens fair in kirtles of the green;
And Anna laid the rock and the weary wheel aside,
    The fairest of the four, I ween.

They're glancing through the glimmer of the quiet eve,
Away in milky wavings of neck and ankle bare;
The heavy-sliding stream in its sleepy song they leave,
    And the crags in the ghostly air.

And linking hand-in-hand, and singing as they go,
The maids along the hillside have ta'en their fearless way,
Till they come to where the rowan trees in lonely beauty grow,
    Beside the Fairy Hawthorn grey.

The Hawthorn stands between the ashes tall and slim,
Like matron with her twin grand-daughters at her knee;
The rowan berries cluster o'er her low head grey and dim
    In ruddy kisses sweet to see.

The merry maidens four have ranged them in a row,
Between each lovely couple a stately rowan stem,
And away in mazes wavy, like skimming birds they go,
    Oh, never carolled bird like them!

But solemn is the silence on the silvery haze
That drinks away their voices in echoless repose,
And dreamily the evening has stilled the haunted braes,
    And dreamier the gloaming grows.

And sinking one by one, like lark-notes from the sky,
When the falcon's shadow saileth across the open shaw,
Are hushed the maidens' voices, as cowering down they lie
    In the flutter of their sudden awe.

For, from the air above and the grassy ground beneath,
And from the mountain-ashes and the old white-thorn between,
A power of faint enchantment doth through their beings breathe,
And they sink down together on the green.

They sink together silent, and stealing side to side,
They fling their lovely arms o'er their drooping necks so fair,
Then vainly strive again their naked arms to hide,
For their shrinking necks again are bare.

Thus clasped and prostrate all, with their heads together bowed,
Soft o'er their bosoms beating—the only human sound—
They hear the silky footsteps of the silent fairy crowd,
Like a river in the air gliding round.

Nor scream can any raise, nor prayer can any say,
But wild, wild the terror of the speechless three—
For they feel fair Anna Grace drawn silently away,
By whom they dare not look to see.

They feel their tresses twine with her parting locks of gold,
And the curls elastic falling, as her head withdraws.
They feel her sliding arms from their trancèd arms unfold,
But they dare not look to see the cause;

For heavy on their senses the faint enchantment lies
Through all that night of anguish and perilous amaze
And neither fear nor wonder can open their quivering eyes,
Or their limbs from the cold ground raise;

Till out of night the earth has rolled her dewy side,
With every haunted mountain and streamy vale below;
When, as the mist dissolves in the yellow morningtide,
The maiden's trance dissolveth so.

Then fly the ghastly three as swiftly as they may,
And tell their tale of sorrow to anxious friends in vain—
They pined away and died within the year and day,
And ne'er was Anna Grace seen again.

Samuel Ferguson
(1810–86)

An Irish fairy doctor could easily detect if a man had lost his soul, for if he had been bargaining with evil spirits the compact was readily detected. At noonday, and even in the brightest sunshine, his body, demoniacally possessed, cast no shadow. Is there here not the implied belief that the shadow was a man's second self, his spirit or his soul? For there are two problems, the solution of which has been attempted in all ages, in all climes, in all creeds, alike by the savage and the philosopher, to ourselves the most important and interesting that can be proposed, namely — So we live after death, and if so, how?

Ulster Journal of Archaeology
Vol. 4, 1898

EXTRACTS FROM THE ISLAND MAGEE WITCH TRAILS

We hear that eight witches were tried at the Assizes at Carrickfergus for bewitching a young gentlewoman, were found guilty and are to be imprisoned for a year and a day and four times pilloried.

THE EXAMINATION OF MARY DUNBAR, TAKEN 12TH MARCH, 1710

Who, being duly Sworn and Examined, Saith that during these Severall weeks she has been in a most grievous and violent manner tormented and afflicted with Witches; that Several whom she never had known, or to her knowledge seen before, did frequently appear to her (tho' invisible to her keepers and attenders), who make her fall very often into fainting and tormenting fitts, take the Power of Tongue from her, and afflicts her to that Degree that she often thinks she is pierced to the heart, and that her breasts are cut off; that she heard the Said women (when about her) name one another, and that called one Jannet Listen, another Eliz. Cellor, another Kate McCamont, another Jannet Carson, another Jannet Mean, another Latimore, and another Mrs. Anne, and the Said Jannet Liston, Eliz. Cellar, Kate McCamont, and Jannet Carson being brought to her, at their first appearance she knew them to be four of her Tormentors, and that after they were taken into Custody the aforesaid Latimore and Mean did very much Torment her, especially when Mr. Sinclare, the Dissenting Minister, was praying with and for her, and told her they would hinder her of hearing his prayers; but if she would do as they would have her, she soon would be well, and that Jannet Latimore and Jannet Mean being brought to her, she likewise knew them to be other two of her Tormentors, and that since the confinement of the said Jannet Liston, Eliz. Cellar, Kate McCamont, Jannet Carson, Jannet Mean, and Jannet Latimor, none of them has troubled her, neither has been so much tormented as when they were at Liberty, and that there do now only two appear to her (viz'-), the aforesaid Mrs. Ann, as they called her, and another woman, blind of an eye, who told her when Mr. Robb, the curate, was going to pray with and for her, that she should be little the better for his prayers, for they would hinder her from hearing them, which they accordingly did.

EDWARD CLEMENTS, Copia Vera.

Dublin Intelligence
April 14th, 1711

AN ESSAY ON WITCHCRAFT

**"Whate'er's in spells, or if there witches be;
Such whimsies seem the most absurd to me."***

Great as the progress of civilization has been during the last century and much as reason has triumphed over superstition through that period, the whole is far from being eradicated and in nought is it more visible than in the belief concerning witchcraft and cows losing their milk or butter by charms and incantations.

The late dreadful catastrophe, in Carnmoney, I thought would have annihilated such superstition, at least in this part of the country, but it seems to have had the contrary effect on those who entertain these strange opinions. It is singular that those said to be adept in this mystic art should be generally old women, who are said to have sold themselves to the devil to obtain a part of his art; they are certainly stupid agents and stupid the devil is if he employs such agents.

Those who believe in such nonsense, say, certain times are more dangerous for witching than others; May-day is accounted very ticklish, as letting fire be taken out of the house on that day would cause some disaster; letting fire be taken out when churning or making cheese is also reckoned very unlucky. I have remarked that a large portion of those people are observers of omens and are raised

---

* from Allan Ramsay, *The Gentle Shepherd* (1725).

KILLING A SUPPOSED WITCH

Illustrated Police News

or depressed in spirits, as they operate on their disordered fancies; for as a late eminent author has justly observed "if you are pleased with prognostics of good, you will be terrified likewise with tokens of evil and your whole life will be a prey to superstition".

To reason with such people as the fore-mentioned is of no use, for if you contradict any of their favourite errors, they instantly call you an unbelieving infidel or some such term. According to these whimsical people, it is very difficult to guard against charms, &c. as they are oft communicated by the eye, in what is commonly called the blink of an ill or evil eye; by this power alone, cows are said to be deprived of their milk, &c. even the human species are said to suffer by this charm. In several parts of England this superstition is prevalent, but there it is necessary for the witch to repeat thrice, I wish, but here, it is said to be done in a moment without any previous words.

The belief of witchcraft is pretty common in most parts of Scotland; a late tourist mentions a person who carved pieces of wood in a curious manner, to be kept in cow-houses as a preservative against charms and every species of witchery. Mr. Boswell also mentions a Mr. M'Queen, a minister of a parish, who preached against such nonsense, with great success; he gave any person leave to take the milk from his cows, provided they did not touch them. This had such an effect that not the least vestige of superstition, in a short time, remained in the parish.

A. Fergus.

Belfast Monthly Magazine
December 1809

—— MRS LOSLIN'S GHOST ——

About the year 1685, Mrs. Charles Loslin, the wife of a farmer, who lived in the parish of Drumbeg, received some violence at the hands of officers of Archdeacon Mathews when serving a warrant upon her husband for tithes, in consequence of which violence she died. Shortly after her death, she appeared several times to a man called Donelson, who had witnessed the treatment she had received and urged him to prosecute a man named Robert Eccleson, by whom the outrage upon her had been committed. This Donelson was unwilling to do so, but the apparition was most urgent in her entreaties and visited Donelson's house several times to induce him to comply with her request.

On one Sunday, she went there several times and (a plain evidence of some invisible power) he was drawn out of their hands in a surprising manner and carried out into the field and yard, she charging him to prosecute justice, which voice, as well as Donelson's reply, these people heard, though they saw no shape. Upon which, the said Donelson deposed what he knew of the violence perpetrated upon Mrs. Loslin before Mr. Rendle Brice, a neighbouring justice, and confirmed all at the assizes, at Down in the year 1685. All this I heard spoken of myself with universal amazement at the time when transacted, living in Belfast at that time, and I should not have been beholden to any to have believed this relation that had been there.

To this Mr. Gilbert, the vicar of Belfast, writing to Baxter about this case, adds — "The matter was notoriously known and believed through the whole country. Nor was there any cause of suspecting any fraud therein, they being all pious, honest neighbours, well-known to me and my parishioners in the parish of Drumbeg, in the County of Down, and Province of Ulster."

Illustrated Police News

When we consider the character and local knowledge of the men who thus testify to the truth of the facts alleged in this case, it is difficult to avoid coming to the conclusion that a better authenticated ghost story could hardly be conceived of than the one which we have now told and of which Mrs. James (Sic) Loslin of Drumbeg was the heroine—

Banbridge Almanac
April 17th, 1886

GHOST AT A MONASTERY
PRIEST'S ASTOUNDING STORY
A BROKEN PROMISE

An extraordinary sensation has been caused in Belfast and district by the declaration made by Father Hubert, the Roman Catholic rector of the Passionist's Church at Ardoyne, that the monastery, which stands close by the church, is haunted.

The declaration was made by the priest in a recent sermon on "The Souls in Purgatory". On retiring to rest a few nights previously, he said a knock came to his bedroom door. A similar knock was heard by another priest in a neighbouring room, and both opened their doors simultaneously. Both saw the figure of a Passionist father pass along the corridor and disappear.

For several nights the ghostly incident was repeated, until, at last, Father Hubert, in the presence of several other Passionist priests, called upon the apparition to speak.

The response came quickly. The ghost, speaking to Father Hubert, said he had not fulfilled a promise made when he (the apparition) was in the flesh to pray for him a certain number of times on certain occasions.

Father Hubert then told the astonished congregation that he had made such a promise to a Passionist father, since dead, whose ghost the apparition was recognised to be by himself and two others of the fathers who had seen it.

He had failed to keep his promise, but since this extraordinary reminder from the other world, prayers had been said for the repose of the soul of the apparition and to the great peace and happiness of the community there. The ghost had not appeared again in the monastery.

In another sermon on the same subject, Father Hubert said the fact that a holy priest had to suffer purgatorial punishment, should cause the people to exercise greater thought and regard for their own dead friends and relatives who might also be in need of their intercession and prayers.

So far from the apparition being startling or sensational, it was not the first, second, or even third visitant from the other world that had been seen in the monastery at Ardoyne.

"In fact," said the rector, "there is not a religious order such as the Passionist community that has not recorded in its annals numbers of instances where ghosts or apparitions have appeared under somewhat similar circumstances.

In conclusion, Father Hubert asserted that he had himself met and interviewed at least two apparitions at other times, but these were not the ghosts of dead clergymen.

Since the sermons were preached, hundreds of persons profoundly influenced by them have been flocking to the church daily to have prayers offered up for repose of the souls of dead friends.

Daily News, London
January 9th, 1906

DERRIAGHY CEMETERY

There are some very grim tales told in connection with Derriaghy, and one is in connection with a past vicar of the parish, although I am not prepared to vouch for the authenticity of the story. It is related that the clergyman was very much disturbed in his mind by a peculiar dream in which the graveyard predominated. He dreamt the same dream on three consecutive nights and, unable to stand the strain any longer, he got up, dressed, and went to the church, which is situated in the middle of the burial ground and there, sure enough, he found a young girl standing at the door. She explained she had come to keep an appointment with her lover. Upon going further the vicar found this man in a secluded part of the grounds busily engaged in digging a grave for his faithful sweetheart, of whom he was anxious to be rid. History does not relate what punishment was inflicted on the would-be murderer, but, if the story be true, it should form a strong argument for those who believe in dream warnings.

'The Silent Land'
Belfast Evening Telegraph
April 13th, 1907

THE "TRINITY STREET GHOST"
SPIRITUALISM INVOKED
WHAT MEDIUM IS SAID TO HAVE REVEALED

Sir Arthur Conan Doyle has "passed on", leaving a number of disciples behind. One of these reached Trinity Street yesterday in the person of Mr. Campbell, a well-known Belfast Spiritualist, who has a firm faith in the Spiritualistic solution of ghost problems.

His accessories included a bag of flour, sealing wax, and a planchette and, with these, the process of laying the ghost, or at any rate of discovering the cause of its unrest, was commenced.

"There is a possibility that these manifestations may be the work of a practical joker," said Mr. Campbell, "so to preclude the chance of further 'take-in', I will make use of this simple trick."

So saying, he took the bag of flour and guided readily, nay, eagerly, by the residents, he proceeded to scatter flour over the stairs leading to the attic whence the ghost was supposed to emerge.

Observe the genius behind Spiritualism, thus disclosed. If a "ghost" of mortal calibre "appeared" there would be tangible evidence of its passing in the condition of the staircase. But, if on the other hand, the ghost were genuine, it would float along leaving no trace on the befloured steps of the stairs.

It was arranged to hold a séance in the front room, just beside the attic. Chairs were arranged. The women, without whom a séance was impossible, were very backward in offering to participate. Mr. Campbell, however, succeeded in inducing one of the women to act as a "medium" and, holding her hand, he exerted his personality and persuasiveness and she appeared to relapse into a trance.

An extraordinary expectancy had been aroused amongst the watchers of this absorbing drama. The séance was held in a closed room and the opening of the door and what it would disclose was awaited with bated breath by a by-this-time "crowded house". When the door at length opened only the IRISH NEWS representative was beckoned into the room.

"Do you know anybody of the name of Edward or Edwards?" asked Mr. Campbell.

"No," I replied. "But why do you ask that?"

In a dramatic whisper he imparted the information that a man of that name had been foully murdered in the house in which we stood. "But where," I cried aghast, "where did the body go?"

Tensely he replied: "Wait without." And the séance was resumed, this time to discover where the body might be.

After some time, I was again beckoned into the room.

"Only one word could be obtained," replied Mr. Campbell gravely, "and that was 'brickyard'."

"Brickyard," I repeated. "Are you sure it was not backyard?"
"We'll try that," said Mr. Campbell, with sudden resolve, and a general trek or perhaps I should say stampede, was made thither.

No brick other than those in the wall could be found in the yard, but, while exploring the coal-hole, Mr. Campbell suddenly dropped on his hands and knees and began scooping away the accumulated garbage.

A brick flooring was revealed, but so soft that it could be scraped with a penknife. Some of the bricks were prised up and, with a knowledge born of his trade as a plasterer, Mr. Campbell informed us that the floor had been laid by an amateur and that there was probably twenty years' difference between the laying of the surrounding walls and the floor. This assertion was based on the difference of the two plasters.

The next step I was informed will be to dig beneath this brick floor. Then, and only then, will it be possible to discover whether the directions given by the "medium" to Mr. Campbell for finding the "body" of the "murdered" "Edwards" were that it lay beneath "bricks" (in the) "yard."

Mr. Campbell is confident that when he initiates his excavation work, he is going to make an interesting discovery. As for me, I merely propose to be there to see what – if anything – he does succeed in unearthing.

Irish News
January 19th, 1932

TRINTY STREET "GHOST"
GIRL SAYS SHE SAW "IT" YESTERDAY POLICE ACTIVITY

About 6 p.m. on Tuesday evening, a girl in the "haunted" house in Trinity Street alleges that she saw the eyes of the "spectre" peering at her through the back window. That, writes an IRISH NEWS representative, is the latest act in the drama that is being enacted in what has now become Belfast's most famous house.

She screamed in terror and, in an instant, Mr. Campbell, the

Spiritualist, was at her side staring intently into the dusky gloom in the yard. He could not see "It" at first, he told me subsequently, but erelong, he added, the eyes of the "spectre" burned their way into his brain – and he saw. Saw a shadowy form, he says, as of a human from the waist upwards. He released the girl, whose arm he was holding, and dashed for the yard.

Here the story was taken up for me by a man who was an eye-witness.

"Mr. Campbell reached the yard," he said, "and we saw him spread-eagled against the wall, as if held there by some invisible force."

Mr. Campbell resumed the tale and graphically related to me how he saw the apparition "floating" up to him until it seemed to merge into his straining eyes. Then, receding rapidly, it passed through the back door.

He followed after it, he says, and falling over the ash-bin, he collapsed against the door.

"I saw the spirit sink into the ground to the left as you come out of the door," he said. "I re-entered the house and then it rose from the floor of the coal shed and I felt its power triumphing over my will. As it sank to the earth whence it came, it irresistibly drew me with it and I felt my knees giving. I could not resist. I thought it had me in its power, when somebody lifted me and I remember no more."

───────────── SPIRITUALIST'S COLLAPSE ─────────────

Any further discoveries that might have been made towards the solution of the "Haunted House Mystery" were nipped in the bud later in the evening by the arrival of the police.

Their anxious inquiries about Mr. Campbell betrayed an interest which cannot have boded well for the Spiritualist, but he intimated by his absence that he had no desire to collide with the law.

The law was baffled, whilst the progress of Spiritualism was baulked.

Irish News
January 20th, 1932

Mr J Arthur Findlay MBE, JP, with Col. Sharman-Crawford
"Survival after Death-
Scientifically Explained."
ULSTER HALL.

THE GHOST

HALF-CLAD peasant lashed his horse
In under the hazel boughs,
An' dashed ower the gravelled clearin'
Afore the ould priest's house.
"Rise, Father John, an' follow me!
Although the night is wild,
My Mary moans her life away
Ower her wee still-born child."

An' Father John O'Donnell heard
That cry o' agony,
An' rose from the hearth, an' crossed himself.
An' closed his Breviary;
An' saddled his horse, an' thro' the night
Raced wi' the frightened clouds
That fled afore the cryin' wind
Like ghosts in gravin'- shrouds.

At Cloughey Hill he met a girl,
She wrung her hands, an' cried:
"Stop, Father John ! You're late! You're late!
Dan Grogan's wife has died."
Her face was ghastly white, her hair
Matted wi' sweat an' rain;
'"May God forbid!" the ould priest called
Again an' yet again.

He urged his horse, an' on an' on
Raced wi' the frightened clouds
That fled afore the wild night wind
Like ghosts in gravin'-shrouds.
He reached the house; the peasant moaned:
"'Twas jist God's Holy Will!
She died aboot the time you'd reached
The foot o' Cloughey Hill."

Padraic Gregory
(1886–1962)

Reputed Ghosts, by Location and Profession:

Amelia	The Crown Bar	Prostitute
Helena Blunden	The Markets	Mill worker/Singer
Biddy	Smithfield	Alcoholic
'Galloper' Thompson	Jennymount	Mill owner
John Savage	Ardilea Street	Property owner
An old woman	John Street (formerly connecting Donegall Street and North Street)	Retired
'Scottie Shoe'	Grand Central Hotel	Gas fitter
Harry & George	Grand Opera House	Stage hands

HISTORY AND NATURAL HISTORY OF REVIVALS

We are told by Archdeacon Stopford that "every girl now struck in Belfast has visions and would think the work only half done if she had not". In these visions, Christ appears in divine splendour. To one fair ecstatic he gives a Gown of Glory; to another, he brings a Suit of Righteousness. Some are struck dumb: one girl is said to have remained speechless for three weeks; another had seventy paralytic seizures in one day. Blindness too is an allotted accompaniment of this epidemic affection. It is instructive to learn that "the friends and bystanders are so persuaded of the miraculous nature of these concomitants that they would resent any attempt to test them".

Spectator, London
December 31st, 1859

THE REVIVAL MOVEMENT IN LISBURN

The "strikings down" and "the marks" vindicated by
Alexander M'Cann, Lisburn, 1859

*"There are more things in heaven and earth, Horatio,
than are dreamt of in your philosophy."– Shakespeare.*

The year 1859 was one of extraordinary mental excitement or
disturbance in the North of Ireland. It was, and is, known as the
year of "The Great Revival". A wave of religious enthusiasm passed
over the country, expressing itself in strange physical phenomena
or manifestations. These manifestations were to a large extent
confined to women. They occurred frequently at religious or
revival meetings and consisted of "Strikings Down", in which
the individual became hysterical, took convulsions, swooned, or
fainted; "The Visions", in which strange revelations were supposed
to be received; and "The Marks".

Many divines and laymen, including the author of "The Year of
Grace" and Alexander M'Cann, believed firmly that the movement
was from above. Others equally reliable, including the Rev. Isaac
Nelson, who wrote "The Year of Delusion"; The Rev. William
Breakey, First Lisburn Presbyterian Church; the Rev. Mr. Hall,
the Cathedral; and the Rev. William Molloy, Methodist minister,
had grave fears that the moving influence might have been from a
different direction.

On one occasion Mr. Breakey and Mr. Hall, hearing of a case,
proceeded to the house to investigate. They found a girl under the
influence and were informed "The Marking" was in progress. The
girl and those present refused to allow "the Marks" to be seen till
they were flushed. The clergymen, however, insisted and saw marks
on the body, but demanding water and soap they washed them off
and left declaring a blue-bag had been used, and that the whole
affair was a fraud.

Lisburn Standard
May 4th, 1917

ON GHOSTS

The present age has been remarkable for the decline of superstition and it is pretty generally acknowledged that good-sense is gaining ground. Yet many remnants of superstition still linger amongst us, owing not a little to the dread that prevails over many, of being called atheists or deists, names which are usually plentifully bestowed on such as oppose common errors, however ridiculous, which have become almost as firm as a creed, from the length of time mankind has believed them.

Among the superstitious relics remaining, we may fairly rank the belief of Ghosts, although few of late years have made much noise in the world.

It is not a little surprising that, in all the stories on record concerning spectres, we never hear a reasonable cause assigned for their appearance, if we except a few, who we are told came to disclose where they had hid their money, doubtless wishing to have their penny a turning. To the appearance of these ghosts few of us, perhaps, would have any objection, but the far greatest part, if we credit the stories handed down to us, appeared with very different views, mostly merely with seeming intention to frighten people: commonly some pious woman, who knew nothing concerning them, till they appeared, uttering a hollow noise, and perhaps all bloody, with their throats cut from ear to ear – "Grinning horribly a ghastly smile".

I remember a by-road near the place in which I lived in infancy, that was well studded with venerable trees on each side, which many good people were timorous to enter after sunset, several persons having related that they had seen, in this place, a black man, driving a fiery chariot, drawn by four black horses! What rendered this story still more surprising and certainly more solemn, was that it was asserted by some, and pretty generally believed, that this charioteer appeared sometimes without his head! In which state we may suppose he cut rather a singular appearance. I have not been able to learn whether he spoke without his head or not!!!

Strange and incredible as it may appear, numerous persons, calling themselves rational beings, believed such nonsense as matters of fact, within these fifty years. For such stuff then formed a larger portion of country fire-side information than at present. Old women and those of the same standard of knowledge, often passing the dreary winter nights in relating terrific fables of ghosts, witches, and murders, which often go hand in hand. I remember, when a boy, being highly delighted with such relations, though they always made me afraid to go to bed, or enter a place that was dark. Sometimes after those tales of terror, I have been so timid as to refrain from looking about, lest I should behold some horrid spectre. And even yet, in spite of scepticism, I am rather afraid to remain in a room without light, which I ascribe to the numerous hobgoblin stories I heard in infancy.

At present many persons are beginning to see the impropriety of telling such stories to children or permitting grannums to frighten them with boggle-boo's. We may, therefore, conclude that the time is not distant when Robin Redy, Stumpy, and numerous others of the same corps will be rarely heard of, even in the fabulous registers of old women.

Belfast Monthly Magazine
August 1812

PHOTOGRAPHING SPIRITS
REMARKABLE SERVICE IN BELFAST CEMETERY

Our Belfast correspondent states that unusual scenes were witnessed at a Service held yesterday at the City Cemetery under the auspices of the local Christian Spiritualists' Association. The Service took place around the grave of Mrs McDermott, mother of Mr John McDermott, medium of the Association, who died about three weeks ago. Upwards of a hundred spiritualists, some of them carrying cameras, were present and during the singing photographs were taken. Mr McDermott conducted the Service, which consisted of prayer, singing and an address.

Mr. Edwin Graham, secretary of the Association, explained that the Service was purely evangelical, and that many photographs had been taken with the object of photographing the spirits of departed friends of persons present at the grave. "It is a very hard thing," he added, "to obtain spirit photographs". He added that when the photographs were developed, in a day or two, they would know whether they had succeeded in their object. Mr Graham explained that a special Service for Mrs McDermott had been held previously in the Hall. She was a native of Glasgow but had been in Belfast for the past year.

Irish Times, Dublin
July 28th, 1926

Samara Leibner

Shortly after this event, John McDermott, the president of the Belfast Christian Spiritualist Association was charged and prosecuted by the Crown. It was found that he, 'did pretend to tell fortunes to deceive and impose on his Majesty's subjects'.

A HISTORY OF THE SPIRITUALIST CHURCH, BY LOCATION

CUSTOM HOUSE SQUARE – It was here, in 1912, at Belfast's forum for public-speaking, that Messrs Morrison, Moore, McCormick, and Skelton first explored and expounded the theology of Spiritualism.

VICTORIA STREET – Those four men agreed to rent a room in Victoria Street, where they could study together and investigate psychic phenomena.

39 HIGH STREET – The Belfast Spiritualist Alliance formed here, holding Sunday meetings in a top floor room.

CENTRAL HALL, ROSEMARY STREET – As interest grew, The Belfast Spiritualist Alliance moved to larger premises at the Central Hall on Rosemary Street. They stayed here until the hall was bombed in an air raid in 1941.

45 MAY STREET – The Spiritualist Alliance then joined forces with a group meeting under the leadership of Sarah Graham, who would become one of the leading figures in Northern Irish Spiritualism.

THOMPSON'S CAFE, 14 DONEGALL PLACE & THOMPSON'S RESTAURANT, 104 EGLANTINE AVENUE – Mr. Thompson was the founder of the Belfast Electronic Spirit Communication Society and the Belfast spiritualists regularly held meetings and services in his cafe and restaurant.

ST. GEORGE'S HALL, 105 HIGH STREET – The Belfast Spiritualist Alliance met regularly here, under the leadership of Joseph Curphy. However, an upstairs drama group and the pools office below caused too much noise and disturbance for satisfactory communion.

6 DUBLIN ROAD – The Belfast Spiritualist Alliance continued here, watched over by Harry Ryding, then living. Their meeting space on the third floor was Curphy Hall in honour of the former president. Many members of the congregation had difficulty climbing the stairs.

134 MALONE AVENUE – On May 4th 1969, The Belfast Church of Psychic Science became the first official Spiritualist church in Ireland. And so it remains.

GEORGE ARTHUR

NORA'S GRAVE
A Tale of Two Lovers

NORAH TATTERSALL.

A fear lest one should utter
Rude words to pain some heart
Or do an action thoughtlessly
To make the tear drops start.
A curbing of the temper
A bridling of the tongue,
When for the good of other souls,
Will make the old seem young.

Then more than faultless features,
And more than golden hair,
Regard the gifts of graciousness,
Oh, maiden, sweet and fair.
That when you go forth duly,
The thought of every mind
Will be — "She is so beautiful,
Because she is so kind."

True, what is youth and beauty,
Bright eyes and tresses fair,
Without the gifts of graciousness,
A gift, alas! Too rare?
But well, too, it becometh,
This tender, thoughtful grace,
This courtesy to all around
The plainest form and face,

The gentle thought for others,
Forgetting self awhile,
The willingness to minister,
And human woe beguile.
The question asked in kindness,
The answer kindly given,
Will give the human countenance
A beauty born in Heaven.

"Love is a dream
Sad is the waking,
Sunshine and sorrow must ever be.
Love is a dream,
Oh would it last forever
For life is so hard
And love is so sweet."

Found on the body
of George Arthur
March 12th, 1890

DESPERATE TRAGEDY AT THE CAVE HILL
A YOUNG MAN SHOOTS HIS SWEETHEART DEAD
AND DIES BY HIS OWN HAND

This morning a young man named Geo. Arthur, aged 26, residing at 150 Nelson Street, Belfast, shot his sweetheart, Nora Tattersell, and afterwards himself. The pair were found about 9 o'clock at the quarries, Cave Hill, the girl quite dead and the man almost at the point of death. His head was reposing upon her breast. Three revolver wounds were in her right temple and one bullet had penetrated the murderer's head. A parcel of cartridges were found beside the couple and a six-chambered revolver.

The young man left his mother's house in Nelson Street last night and did not return. It is stated that he had been in the habit of going to see his sweetheart regularly and was supposed to have gone last night on a similar errand. Circumstances transpired which prevented his marriage with his sweetheart. When found at the quarries by a workman, who conveyed the intelligence of the tragedy to the Ligoneil barracks, he was at once conveyed to the Royal Hospital, where he died at about 11.30 — five minutes after his admission.

Belfast Evening Telegraph
March 12th, 1890

MELANCHOLY LOVE AFFAIR
A YOUNG MAN MURDERS HIS SWEETHEART

The leading facts regarding the very painful occurrence can be briefly stated. George Arthur, the young man who murdered his sweetheart and then committed suicide, has been for two and a half years in the employment of Messrs. G. & J. Burns, Queen's Square, as a clerk. On Tuesday, he asked permission to remain away after dinner hour and this concession was promptly granted to one whose conduct with the employers has been always commendable and who was quite a favourite with his companions in the counting-house.

During the past six months he had been intimate with the

young woman who, unhappily, has lost her life. She has, for that period, been his sweetheart. Her name was Nora Tatersall and she was employed as a domestic servant in the residence of Mr. Best, 3 Clarence Place, May Street.

This girl, it seems, was a native of Dublin, but had resided for some time in England. During twenty months she had been a servant with Mr. and Mrs. Best, who speak of her in very favourable terms, both as to her character and amiable manners. In consequence of the work in that household being, as she considered, somewhat too heavy, she had decided upon leaving and securing a situation in a family where the labour would be lighter.

There is no doubt that, for the past month her conduct was considered to be rather erratic. We understand that, on Tuesday, she playfully said to one of the children that she was going to be shot by her sweetheart, but no notice was taken of the remark, which was merely considered part of her childish talk to the little one.

As soon as the intelligence of the shocking tragedy became known in the city, large numbers wended their way to the spot for the purpose of obtaining a view of the body and this continued up till the time of its removal.

In the possession of Arthur were found a box of cartridges corresponding in every particular with the revolver and four lengthy letters, three of which were written in a fine, round hand, admittedly that of Arthur himself, the remaining epistle being in a female hand addressed to Arthur and bearing the signature of the young woman.

TO THE EDITOR OF THE EVENING TELEGRAPH

No one must ever blame dear Nora for what has occurred. It has not been her fault. We love each other, but circumstances have happened in the past which prevent our union and, by mutual agreement, we have consented to die rather than continue to live in this weary world. I am sorry to take her life, but alas! There is no alternative. God forgive me. Never was there such a good, tender-hearted angel born in this world before.

The coroner's jury may return their usual verdict of temporary insanity, but I am not even temporarily insane; on the contrary, I am clothed in my right mind.

Nora, darling, farewell until we meet on the opposite side of the river. You remember what I wrote you once before, dear, in the words of Byron, I think—

I cannot lose a world for thee,
But would not lose thee for a world.
God forgive me and bless my own dear Nora,

George

P.S.— There is too much work for one at those ledger accounts.

3 Clarence Place,
December 11th, 1889

Dear George,
I am so sorry for fretting you last night. If you knew
the state of my mind, you would forgive me for getting
into such a temper. It makes me so miserable to see you
wasting your time coming down to see me when I know that
I am anything but worthy of you. There is a great barrier
which my feelings prevent me telling you, either by word or
letter, but some day perhaps you will know. I won't go out
on a wet night again, as I got cold last night and I have
been suffering from neuralgia all day. Like a good child,
don't come down before Friday night, about 9.30 p.m. I was
greatly pleased to see you lately, so steady. I must now
say good bye as I have a heater in the fire and if I don't
go soon it will melt.

Your fool,
Nora

49 Queen's Square
March 11th, 1890.

My own Darling,
I have come into the office simply to drop you a few lines. I
do not wish to stay here very long, so that I can only say
a few words to you. I have kept my promise to you and have
not tasted any drink to-day, so that my head is perfectly
clear and I am very happy in the knowledge that we both die
together. Be cheerful, darling, and keep up your spirits
until I come round at seven o'clock.
    How I long for the time when I shall see you again. I
wonder will it be for the last time. No, it cannot be so,
for truly the good Lord will let us meet again in the next
world. God bless you, my own bonnie; God bless you – Yours
true till death.

George

Northern Whig
March 13th, 1890

ADDITIONAL INCIDENTS OF THE TRAGEDY

Further inquiries in Belfast have resulted in the discovery that George Arthur and Miss "Tattersell" took first-class tickets on Tuesday evening by the 7.30 train. They took their seats in the first-class compartment and their demeanour showed that they wished to be left by themselves. This however was not to be as one or two other persons entered this compartment before the trip started. They were seen returning from Whiteabbey, but the train was due at 9.35 and it was after that that they were seen in York Street when Miss "Tattersell" was crying.

It was on their return as far we can learn that they visited a fruiterer's shop where oranges were purchased by Arthur and handed over to Miss "Tattersell." Their movements after were not observed by any person who knew them and the next thing that was heard of them was the finding of the bodies at the Cave Hill.

Belfast Evening Telegraph
March 14th, 1890

THE FUNERAL

Yesterday, the remains of the unhappy pair whose lives came to a close on Wednesday morning, under such tragic circumstances, were interred in the City Cemetery. As had been arranged on Thursday, both bodies have been placed in the same grave. This may be said to be quite in keeping with the romantic manner in which their lives were sacrificed.

The procession started for the City Cemetery; it was reached about half-past eleven o'clock. Long before the hour many people had found their way to the final resting place of the ill-starred lovers. Groups of girls were gathered here and there, eagerly discussing the untimely fate of those whose funeral they awaited. The sympathisers included, too, quite a number of women with children mewling and squealing in their arms, hospital nurses in their curious navy blue uniforms, a select company of Highlanders in their kilts and a lot of juveniles who were doubtless attracted thither more by curiosity than anything else.

The Rev. John Spence, M.A. (Mariners' Episcopal Church), with whose congregation the Arthur family are connected, conducted service. He also delivered an address on the words "It

is appointed unto men once to die, but after this the judgment"
(Hebrews, 9th chap., 27th verse).

Northern Whig
March 15th, 1890

REV. JOHN SPENCE

I don't suppose it is possible for anyone to conceive of our meeting
under more trying circumstances in which we are met together here
to-day. I am quite sure a very large number of those here present
this morning have come to show their sympathy with the family or
families that are passing through this terrible sea of trial and trouble
and that our prayers to God are that they may be sustained and
comforted in this overwhelming calamity that has befallen them.

At the same time, I cannot help noticing that it is just possible that
many are here today simply influenced by a morbid sentimentality
– not for anything they can see or anything they can hear – but
just because there is something sensational going on and they wish
to share in that sensation. If I am wrong, God forgive me for the
uncharitableness; if I am right, God forgive those who are yielding
to such base sentiment and gratifying such an unholy carnal feeling
and giving way to such an improper excitement.

Belfast News-Letter
March 15th, 1890

LUCIDATING THE MYSTERY
CONTINUED EXCITEMENT IN BELFAST

It is apparent that the absorbing interest taken in this terrible
affair is not by any means on the wane. Yesterday, a large number
of people visited the scene of the dreadful love tragedy at the base
of the Cave Hill and also the grave in the City Cemetery where
the remains of the lovers were interred. The police still continue
the investigation with reference to the antecedents of Nora
"Tattersell," but up to the present their efforts have been attended
with little or no success.

This is about the sum total of what has been definitely
ascertained as to her past career, but there are rumours in
circulation possessing as far as can been seen but little foundation.
One of them, however, which may be mentioned and which we give

for what it is worth is that Nora Tattersell, or whatever her correct name may be, was married to a sea captain. Whether this is a fact or not cannot be decided with the information at present to hand, but if it should be true it would no doubt throw a great deal of light upon the statement in her letter to her lover to the effect that she was unworthy of him and that there was a barrier to their union which she could not disclose.

Belfast Evening Telegraph
March 17th, 1890

THE MYSTERY DEEPENS

The rumour which has currently circulated in the city yesterday that a brother of the deceased girl was in the Metropolitan Force in Dublin proves to be unfounded, as the following telegram received by Sergeant Farrell this morning, testifies:

"No sergeant or constable named Tattersell here. A sergeant named Patterson served here some years ago but he knows nothing of the name. He resides at 33 Upper Canal Street.

SGT. WHITTAKER, Police Station, Lad Lane, Baggott Street."

It is now generally believed that the name "Nora Tattersell" was an assumed one.

Belfast Evening Telegraph
March 13th, 1890

AUTHENTIC HISTORY OF THE GIRL'S LIFE

The Lurgan Mail, a new weekly journal in Lurgan, says: in relation to the history of this peculiar young woman, facts have come to our knowledge which at once pronounce her a person of romance and mystery. Through a young woman with whom she was on terms of familiarity in Portadown, we learn that the deceased was a person of very superior accomplishments and evidently living beneath her station in life. She was highly educated and undertook the musical tuition of the children of the family she lived with. Her own statement was that she was the child of a constabulary inspector who was killed. She never alluded to her mother or her home, but alleged that she was trained under Miss Skinner, the governess for whom Dr. Cross* murdered his wife; and she resided as a servant in Shandy Hall, Cork, with Dr. Cross.

She was a person of impulsive temperament and often, when teaching on the piano in Portadown, she would burst suddenly into tears and break down under the emotions of some past recollection, which she never disclosed. Both in Portadown and Lurgan, she manifested a strong attachment for the opposite sex and could scarcely be kept under proper restraint. Her religious belief is, like her birth, a mystery, as she never professed any form of faith but was passionately fond of light literature and romance and was often heard to look forward to Belfast as the home of her destiny.

Belfast Evening Telegraph
March 17th, 1890

THE BELFAST LOVE TRAGEDY
INTERVIEW WITH NORA TATTERSELL'S AUNT

Our Midleton (County Cork) correspondent telegraphs: –

Seeing in your issue of Saturday, in connection with the recent tragedy at Belfast, that the victim, Nora Tattersell was stated to have an aunt living in the town, I thought it my duty, as your representative here, to look up the matter and try and establish the fact.

Despite many difficulties, I succeeded before long in finding out the aunt of Nora Tattersell. She had heard nothing and knew nothing of the awful tragedy at Belfast. After I had put her in possession of some of the circumstances of the affair, she explained to me that she had a niece named Nora McCarthy, who probably had taken her mother's name of Harte. That would account for her being known as Nora Harte. Nora had a stepfather called Tattersell and, perhaps too, she was known on that account as Nora Tattersell.

Nora lived with her father and mother in Cork City, here her father died. Nora was but a child then and was reared by her grandmother and was kept well to school. Nora was an intelligent, little girl and was known and still remembered here as Nora Harte. In the course of a few years, her grandmother died. Her aunt got married to her husband and Nora,

---

* Dr. Philip Cross (1826–88) was the perpetrator in the Coachford Poisoning Case. Living in Shandy Hall, Dripsey, County Cork, he was convicted and hanged for the murder, by poisoning, of his wife, after an affair with his children's governess.

being grown up to womanhood, went to earn her bread.

It was nearly seven years since Nora had left Midleton. In that period Nora had written to her aunt two or three times. She remembers nothing definite about those letters, where they were written from or the contents thereof, except the last letter Nora wrote her, which she received last Christmas two years from some town in the County Armagh. She had not preserved these letters.

As it appeared in your issue on Saturday that the police authorities here were communicated with on the matter, I asked the aunt if she had been visited by the constabulary on the subject. She said not. The interview then closed. I have ascertained that the police made exclusive inquiries over the town, but all to no avail in finding the proper person.

─────── **THE BARRIER IN THE CASE** ───────

The 'Freeman's Journal' to-day says — it appears that the barrier to the union of George Arthur and Nora Tattersell was the fact that some time ago she was married to an old man, now resident in London, but from whom she had been separated for some time. The girl fell desperately in love with Arthur and the affection was reciprocated, but the thought that the marriage could not take place preyed strongly upon the minds of both.

Belfast Evening Telegraph
March 18th, 1890

NORA'S GRAVE

'Tis a tale of love and wild romance
When Cupid dared to bend
His mighty bow and to fan the flame
Of devouring love, when Nora came
To her sad and tragic end.

Let Nora sleep by her lover's side
Nor their dreadful deed condemn
For weak and frail is the human heart
When Cupid wings his fiery dart
The world was not for them.

Anon.

THE
CAVE
HILL

*O*n a fair day, from the top of Cave Hill — Ben Madigan to some — one can see the Isle of Man, the Mull of Galloway, and Carrick. On a rainy, dull, or damp day, one sees only Belfast, caught in the valley by the long shadow of the hill.

Cave Hill is the far-reaches and the wilds, the setting for forbidden meetings, unlikely allegiances, and desperate escapes. So, while the city pushes its shadow-self further and further from the centre, the shadow rises up and falls back onto the city.

WOLF AT AUGHNABRACK

In 1825, J. Compton, a schoolmaster in Telfairs Entry, Belfast, brought out a little book entitled A Compendious System of Chronology, printed by Joseph Smyth. Under the year 1612, he gives the following item: "The last wolf seen in Ireland is killed with Irish wolf-dogs on the hill of Aughnabrack, near Belfast, by Clotworthy Upton, of Castle-Upton, Templepatrick."

Aughnabrack lies behind the present Wolfhill, which local tradition has long associated with the wolf.

Ulster Journal of Archaeology
Volume 2, 1894

AT BELLEVUE ZOO

Mr Richard Foster, Head Keeper at Bellevue Zoo, with a 12-weeks-old pig, which is causing quite a lot of amusement owing to its smallness in size. It should be by right about six times as large.

Northern Whig
October 14th, 1937

THE TABLE BOOK

OR, DAILY RECREATION AND INFORMATION CONCERNING REMARKABLE MEN, MANNERS, TIMES, SEASONS, SOLEMNITIES, MERRY-MAKINGS, ANTIQUITIES AND NOBILITIES, FORMING A COMPLETE HISTORY OF THE YEAR.

"On the same day several thousands of the working classes of the town and vicinity of Belfast, County Antrim, resort to the Cave-hill, about three miles distant, where the day is spent dancing, jumping, running, climbing the rugged rocks and drinking. Here many a rude brawl takes place, many return home with black eyes and bloody noses, and in some cases with broken bones. Indeed it is with them the greatest holiday of the year, and to not a few it furnishes laughable treats to talk about, till the return of the following spring. On this evening a kind of dramatic piece is usually brought forward at the Belfast theatre, called 'The Humours of the Cave-hill'."

William Hone
1827

The Cave Hill

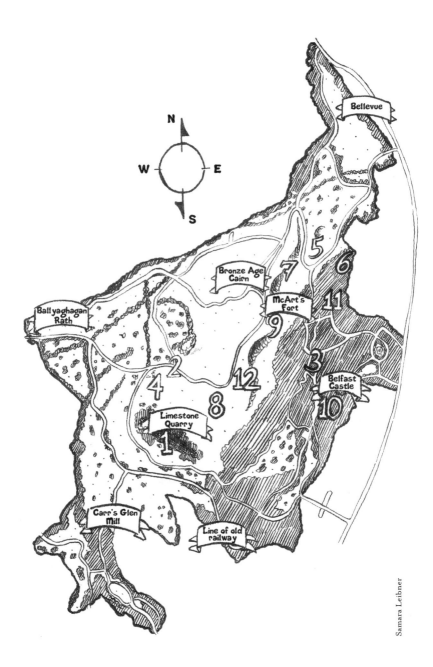

N
W E
S

Bellevue

Bronze Age
Cairn

5

7

6

Ballyaghagan
Rath

McArt's
Fort

9

11

2

3

4

12

8

Belfast
Castle

1

Limestone
Quarry

10

Carr's Glen
Mill

Line of old
railway

Samara Leibner

KEY

1.   The place where George and Nora died in 1890.

2.   In 1899, Maude Gonne had a vision here, when visiting the
     Cave Hill with Yeats.

3.   *Adoxa moschatellina*, the rarest plant in Ireland, grows on this
     spot, blooming once a year, in April.

4.   The site of the Cave Hill Diamond.

5.   The Devil's Punchbowl.

6.   In 1807, three people died here, suffocated by the 'sulphurous
     smoke' of a local sorceress.

7.   Site of brigandry and highway robbery in the seventeenth and
     eighteenth century.

8.   The meeting spot of Henry Joy McCracken and his lover
     Mary Bodel.

9.   The meeting place of the United Irishmen in 1795.

10. The bell tower of Belfast Castle, where Jimmie the baboon
     was found ringing the bell, after he escaped from the zoo
     in 1935.

11. The preacher James Stewart's house, where a fast was held, in
     1672, to rid him of a ghost.

12. The spot where, in March 1922, an unidentifiable skeleton
     was found wearing a black overcoat with velvet collar. In the
     pockets were an Arabic coin, a small copper coin, an
     autograph case and a pocket book containing pulp material
     which had probably been bank notes.

A PAGAN HYMN

Beauty may mock when we are dumb,
And joy find us expressionless,
And passion clothe us like a dress,
When words, for calling, will not come.

Sing dirges to the waning moon,
And hymn the dawn with due lament;
While silence holds the firmament
Thou shalt not draw forth rhyme or rune.

Catch the sea spray upon your lips,
And glut your eyes on surge and swell.
And let tempestuous voices yell
In frenzy for the death of ships.

Spread the calm waters like a sheet
Of burnished copper to the West:
Make Evening's glory manifest,
And feel day's dying pulses beat.

Watch the new opened eyes of heaven
Gaze calmly on a warring world.
And see the lips of Saturn curled.
Most ominous of the Sacred Seven.

Call dreams to fill your slumbering brain;
Lay scroll and pen beside your bed;
Walk pleasant meadows with the dead,
And claim secession of your pain.

Struggle no more; but wait thine hour,
And grasp the gift that hour must bring;
So shall the bells of beauty ring,
And whispers pass from flower to flower.

And when the moon hath climbed her throne
Lead forth thy beauty to the hills,
Follow some rivulet which fills
A lake with lilies overgrown.

Then stand upon the weedy brim,
And let the silent waters show
The secret which your soul would know;
And chant the Danann's ancient hymn,

To lure from out the glittering deep
Love's ultimate reflected light.
Then get you gone into the night,
And pass unto the gates of sleep.

Herbert Moore Pim
(1883–1950)

TOBY IS DEAD

A Pagan Game for Children

Poor Toby is dead and he lies in his grave.
Lies in his grave, lies in his grave.
Poor Toby is dead and he lies in his grave,
Lies in his grave, lies in his grave.

They planted an apple tree over his head,
Over his head, over his head.
They planted an apple tree over his head,
Over his head, over his head.

The apples grew ripe and they all fell off,
All fell off, all fell off.
The apples grew ripe and they all fell off,
All fell off, all fell off.

There came an old woman picking them up,
Picking them up, picking them up.
There came an old woman picking them up,
Picking them up, picking them up.

Poor Toby gets up and he gave her a clout,
Gave her a clout, gave her a clout.
Poor Toby gets up and he gave her a clout,
Gave her a clout, gave her a clout.

He makes the old woman go hippity hop,
Hippity hop, hippity hop.
He makes the old woman go hippity hop,
Hippity hop, hippity hop.

Samara Leibner

Upon the 23rd of March, at 5.10 o'clock in the morning, two constables, in different parts of the city of Peterborough, had reported having seen an object, carrying a light, moving over the city, with sounds like the sounds of a motor. In the Peterborough Advertiser, March 27th, is published an interview with one of these constables, who described "an object, somewhat oblong and narrow in shape, carrying a powerful light". To suit whatever anybody should prefer, I could give data to show that only lights, and no object were seen, and that no sound was heard; or that a vessel, carrying lights, was seen, and that sounds, like sounds of a motor, were heard.

It is said, in the Daily Mail, May 17th, that many other stories of unaccountable objects and lights in the sky had reached the office of the Mail. If so, the stories were not published.

The range of the reported observations was from Ipswich, on the east coast of England, to Belfast, Ireland, a distance of 350 miles. Perhaps a gas bag could be dragged around a little, but the imitation-airship that was found at Dunstable, was a flimsy contrivance, consisting of two hot-air balloons, and a frame about 20 feet long, connecting them. The lights in the sky were frequently reported, upon the same night, from places far apart.

Lo!
Charles Fort
1931

DR. BOYD'S AIRSHIP
A MYSTERY EXPLAINED

The London Daily News representative has interviewed the inventor of the "phantom" airship which some months ago caused so much alarm and excited so much incredulity in the East of England and in South Wales. The airship, it is stated, is at present lying in a private park, little more than an hour's ride from London. Dr. M.B. Boyd, the owner and inventor, has been perfecting this invention for eight years, but only began his trials in March last. He continued them by night with the utmost secrecy throughout April and May. If Dr. Boyd has accomplished, adds the journal, all that he claims to have done — and he states that he has plenty of witnesses and documents to prove it — England has little cause to fear falling behind in the race for aerial supremacy.

In the interview, Dr. Boyd stated that in May he began to travel long distances and his achievements became sufficiently known to be exaggerated by rumour. On May 18th came news from Belfast that inhabitants had witnessed "the flight of a dark body bearing a brilliant light, which passed over the city at a great height".*

ACROSS THE IRISH CHANNEL

"That was the occasion when we accomplished our longest flight," said Dr. Boyd. "On that night, we flew across the Irish Channel and I have plenty of proof of the fact. Where we crossed the distance from shore to shore is about ninety miles. We accomplished the journey in one night, in one long continuous flight and we attained an average speed of thirty-two miles an hour.

---

* Some reports suggest that the ship landed in the hills surrounding Belfast and that the strange crew disembarked.

"Unlike the usual form of airship, it has no car suspended from the envelope, neither is the envelope exactly cigar-shaped, but rather oval and is divided into three separate bags. The works are placed between them, the motors having a closed-in compartment to themselves at the end. From each side extend wings like an aeroplane."

FEATURES OF THE SHIP

"The ship is 120 feet long and has engines of 300 horse-power — a great difference from the Zeppelin airship, which is 446 feet long, and has engines of only 220 h.p. Another feature is the number of propellers. There are four on the machine at present, and these can be increased to any number up to thirty-two."

London Daily News
June, 1909

DR. BOYD'S AIRSHIP
A NEWSPAPER HOAXED
REASON NOT STATED

Some days ago the "Daily News" was responsible for a story to the effect that a Dr. M. Boyd had made nocturnal flights in an airship of his own design and construction across the Irish Channel to near Belfast and back again to England; that this airship, which travelled at the height of 3500 feet, was the mysterious airship reported to have been seen at several places; and that a company was being formed to work the invention.

The "Daily Chronicle", this morning, declares the whole story to be a pure fabrication and quotes as its authority the so-called Dr. Boyd himself — real name not given — with whom one of its staff had an interview. "Dr. Boyd," it says, "admits that he palmed off the story on the 'Daily News' as a hoax, but his motive for doing so is not stated."

Kalgoorlie Miner, Australia
July 13th, 1909

A HOAX
FLIGHT TO BELFAST
SO-CALLED DR. BOYD

By Electric Telegraph (received July 13th, 8.25am)
London, July 12th — The previous cable stated that a private syndicate,

with a capital of £250,000, was being formed to work Dr. M. Boyd's airship. With two companions, Dr. Boyd crossed the Irish Channel, with the utmost secrecy, at night time, last March, at a height of 3500ft., in four hours, the distance being ninety miles, and landed near Belfast, recrossing the following night. Dr. Boyd admitted that his airship was the mysterious one reported to have been seen hovering over Caerphilly and Cardiff (Wales), Northampton, and elsewhere a few months ago.

Taranaki Herald, New Zealand
July 13th, 1909

Samara Leibner

∞ *THE CRUISE OF THE SCARESHIP* ∞

Which I wish to remark
And my language is plain
That for ways that are dark
And for tricks that are vain,
The aeroplane's deuced peculiar —
Which the same I would rise to maintain.

"Spotted Gull" was its name;
And its owner one night
Softly took out the same,
And was fixing the kite,
When the beastly thing bucked and flew upwards,
And vanished — at least from HIS sight.

But that airship was seen
With a crew and with none,
And was blue, red, or green
Ere the next day was done.
That unfortunate multi-sized airship
In some half-dozen counties was seen.

Over Lincolnshire fens,
It had Germans on board;
And Glamorganshire glens
Saw the flash of a sword.
While over in Belfast the gossoons
By French curses from Heaven were awed.

Many folk know the craze
For the "nocturnal flight"
So that airship still plays
To two houses a night.
Doing turns to the folk in East Anglia,
And doubling for Cardiff's delight.

'Puck'
The Daily Chronicle
1909

THE BOTANIC GARDENS

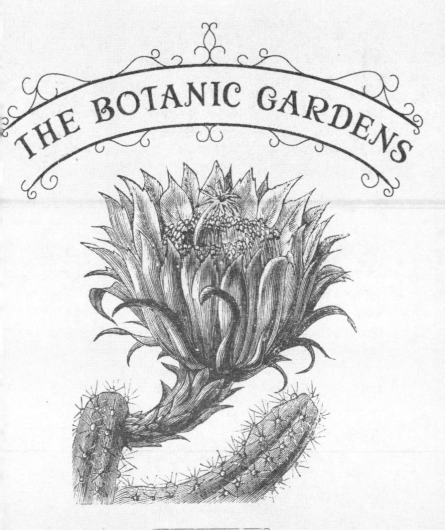

CEREUS GRANDIFLORUS

The green expanse of the Botanic Gardens was opened in 1828, a private paradise for subscribers and members of the Belfast Botanic and Horticultural Society, who cultivated beauty and contemplation in its grounds. It was not seen this way by everyone however: a group of pious city fathers protested against it through the 1840s, with the good Dr Cook decrying it as 'The Sunday Trap', another contrivance of Satan to distract Christians from the Sabbath. The working classes didn't see the gardens at all until 1865, and this only through the benevolent efforts of Dr Wyville Thomson and Mr Nicholas Grimshaw. It was thus that everyone got to see such wonders as Cavier the Dancing Bear, The Grand Exhibition of the North East of Ireland Bee Keepers Association, and Rivalli the Fire-Proof Man and it was thus that many of Belfast's citizens wasted Sunday.

THE ROYAL BOTANIC GARDENS

WILL OPEN AT NIGHT

that subscribers may witness, for the first time, the night flowering of

CEREUS GRANDIFLORUS

JUNE 1847

CURATOR'S REPORT

A serious obstacle I have to contend with in these outlying parts of the grounds is the mischievous conduct of the young visitors. Instead of appreciating the Garden as they ought, they show by their thoughtlessness a more destructive tendency than was evinced twenty-five years ago. I would, therefore, implore parents to use their influence with their children and urge them to refrain from injuring the property of the Garden.

Your most obedient Servant,

Daniel Ferguson

December 31st, 1862

We are not of those who fear to trust working people: what we would ask every working man who takes his family to the Gardens to do would be to discountenance and aid in repressing everything of that disruptive nature: to have pride of class in contributing to general order and decorum, and to promptly put down, by appeal to the authority which will be at hand, every symptom of a disorderly spirit.

Northern Whig
April 2nd, 1865

BLONDIN! BLONDIN!

ROYAL BOTANIC GARDENS,
BELFAST.

FRIDAY, AUGUST 16, 1861.

THE RENOWNED BLONDIN, THE HERO
of Niagara, the King of the Tight Rope, and the
Wonder of the World, will make his astounding and
perilous
CATARACT ASCENSION
ON A
ROPE 100 FEET HIGH AND 500 FEET LONG,
On FRIDAY, 16th August,
IN THE BOTANIC GARDENS, BELFAST.

Bands will be in attendance.
Tickets of Admission— Previous to the Day of Exhi-
bition—To Non-Subscribers, 1s 6d ; Subscribers, 1s.
On the Day—All Tickets, 2s each.

Mercantile Journal
August 13th, 1861

BLONDIN AT THE BOTANIC GARDENS

Yesterday afternoon, M. Blondin, "The Hero of Niagara, the king of the Tight Rope, and the Wonder of the World", made his "astonishing and perilous Cataract ascent" at the Botanic Gardens, in view of about 7,000 persons, many of whom had come into town by excursion trains from distant parts of the province for the purpose of seeing this prince of acrobats.

It was announced that the rope on which M. Blondin would make his ascent would be 100 feet high and 500 feet long, instead of which it was 65 feet from the ground and the entire length did not exceed 300 feet. The wooden posts which supported it were firmly fixed in the ground and secured by numerous "stays". At the top of each was a sort of seat, over which the rope – a very strong hempen one, about two inches in diameter – passed and it was tightened by means of a windlass. At equal distances of about thirty feet throughout the entire length, smaller ropes, with sandbags at the end and fastened to the ground by wooden pegs, were attached, so as to steady it and make it less liable to yield when pressed upon by the foot.

M. Blondin made his appearance at twenty minutes to four o'clock. He was dressed in the ordinary garb of an acrobat and wore on his breast two large gold medals, which were presented to him on the other side of the Atlantic in token of admiration of his wonderful feats.

He bowed his acknowledgments to the spectators below and, taking up his heavy balancing pole, he prepared to start on his perilous journey. He proceeded very slowly and cautiously down the

Samara Leibner

steepest part of the rope and gave the spectators the idea that the feat was one that cost him much exertion, but, after he had got over a few yards, he ran along quickly and did not stop till he was on the centre of the rope.

At this stage of the proceedings, the sky became overcast and a heavy shower of rain began to descend. The spectators took shelter under the trees or under umbrellas, but Blondin, although wet to the skin, and with the rope made slippery and terribly dangerous, did not give up.

At the middle of the rope, he again stopped and fastened his balancing pole to it by means of a cord, after which he performed various feats — such as standing on his head on the pole and throwing somersaults backwards, with great apparent ease and confidence.

M. Blondin may hope to increase the interest of his exhibition by staggering, trembling, and pretending to miss the rope with his foot when he crosses it blindfolded — and with the astonishing power he possesses he can probably make these apparent blunders with perfect safety to himself, but few who witness his feats care to see the simulation of difficulty and doubt. If M. Blondin can do what other acrobats cannot do, his superiority is not less decided because he does it easily and surely. The manner in which, after the first few yards, he ran along the rope blindfolded, stood on one leg, stretched himself on the rope, &c., showed that he was a perfect master of the art.

Arrived at the other end of the rope, he removed the sack and handkerchief and threw them down to be examined by those below. A tall, full-grown man, much larger in every way than M. Blondin, was then hoisted to the cradle and mounted on the daring acrobat's back and, burdened in this way, he set out to recross the rope. This feat was witnessed with astonishment by the crowds below. The rope, which the rain had loosened instead of tightening, was very slippery and yielded considerably to the weight of the two men. It swayed a little backwards and forwards and M. Blondin stopped for an instant till the motion lessened and then resumed his course. The man upon his back — the same, we are informed, that crossed the Niagra Falls with him — displayed great nerve and preserved an impassability which was very surprising under the circumstances. The slightest motion on his part — the slightest alteration of his position — would have brought both of them to the ground and with what result may easily be imagined.

The remainder of the journey was got over apparently as easily as if he had been walking on terra firma. M. Blondin then descended and it was with great difficulty that his enthusiastic admirers were prevented from chairing him.

The sky again cleared up and the sun shone forth with great brilliancy. A large number of the visitors remained to witness the magical entertainments of Mdlle Veroni*, but many who had come from a distance by railway left immediately for home. M. Blondin will give another and last performance in the Gardens to-day.

Found among the annual reports of
The Belfast Botanic and Horticultural Society
August 16th, 1861

Charles Blondin (1824–97), an internationally renowned tightrope walker and acrobat, famed for his crossing of Niagara Falls, during which he would, at the midway point, cook and eat an omelette. After a faulty rope in Dublin caused the deaths of two scaffolding workers, he used ropes from the Belfast Ropeworks exclusively for the remainder of his career. He performed in Belfast many times and, in 1896, gave his final ever professional performance there at the age of 72, while blind in one eye.

The curator still has to complain of injuries done by parties, particularly juveniles, to the shrubs, flowers, &c., and the pilfering of cuttings of plants. This became so general that a watchman had to be employed and two parties were detected and had to pay smart fines. The board are resolved for the future to maintain a constant watch, in order to prosecute the parties publicly who are guilty of such misconduct.

A letter was read from Mr. Robert E. Hunter, an agent, Belfast, asking upon what terms he could have the use of the gardens for a Grand Fete and exhibition of fireworks. Mr. Lee was instructed to inform Mr. Hunter that fireworks being a large portion of the entertainment, they decline to let the Gardens, believing that they would be much injured by a night entertainment.

Minutes of the Belfast Botanic and Horticultural Society
July 18th, 1864

---

* Famously, Britain's only female magician.

NOTICE

THE PROPRIETORS OF THE ROYAL BOTANIC GARDENS and the Public generally, having frequently expressed a wish that Flower Shows in connection with the ROYAL BOTANIC COMPANY (Limited) should still be held, although the Company has met with heavy losses by these shows, the Directors are still unwilling that any object which so much tends to advance and refine public taste should be discontinued without making a final effort and they have accordingly arranged that, if a sufficient Prize Fund can be secured to cover expenses, a grand Autumn Show will be in held in August next.

Subscription Lists will be opened and copies left in the Banks and News-Room and Eight Tickets, giving early admission to the Show, will be given to every Subscriber for each £1 subscribed. Should a sufficient sum not be generated before the 1st MAY, the Show will not be held.

GEO. A. CARRUTHERS, Secretary.
ROYAL BELFAST BOTANIC AND HORTICULTURAL COMPANY (LIMITED),
52, WARING STREET
April 12th, 1864

GRAND FETE CHAMPETRE
at the
ROYAL BOTANIC GARDENS
ON
MONDAY, THE 9th JUNE,
ON WHICH OCCASION
DR. MARK AND HIS LITTLE MEN
WILL APPEAR AT
TWO GRAND CONCERTS

GREAT BALLOON ASCENT

On Thursday evening, Mr. Coxwell, the celebrated aeronaut, made an ascent from the Royal Botanic Gardens in his new mammoth balloon, which he has called the "Britannica". This balloon is announced as the largest in the world. It is 100 feet in height and requires 100,000 cubic feet of gas to inflate it. It is many years since there was a balloon ascent in this town and this circumstance,

Samara Leibner

together with the well-known eminence of Mr. Coxwell as an aerial voyager and the brilliancy of the weather, gave to the speculation a degree of interest far exceeding anything we have had here for a long period.

The occupants of the balloon, eleven in number, were the following: Mr. Coxwell; Captain Matthew Hale, Cameronians; Captain Tullock, 96th Regiment; Mr. Rowan, 62d Regiment; Mr. Douthwaite and Mr. Sharp, Cameronians; Mr. Alexander P.

Henderson, University Square; Mr. Alexander Porter, University Square; Mr. Robert Kingan, a gentleman from Armagh, and Dr. Corry, Clarendon Place. Mr. Alexander F. Herdman, Donegall Square South; and Mr. George M'Tear, Jnr., Carilise Terrace, were also anxious to go up and were in the car for that purpose, but Mr. Coxwell considered that eleven was the greatest number he could safely allow to ascend.

The following is an account of the voyage by one of the gentlemen who made the ascent:

THE JOURNEY

Anyone who has witnessed the start for the Derby St. Leger or any other of the great English races will know something of the excitement of the crowd and the feverish anxiety of those interested in the event and the longing for the flag to be dropped and the start to be made. To a very considerable extent, this was the feeling of the occupants of the "car" of Mr. Coxwell's balloon, as they waited anxiously for the minute when the crowd which pressed around on every side would fall back and enable the balloon to get a fair chance for its ascent.

The spectacle, as we left the Gardens, was one of the most extraordinary it is possible to conceive. The upturned faces of many thousand people, as they watched us start on what most thought a perilous journey, was for an instant a perfect study, but we soon rose clear above them and even lost the majestic strain of our National Anthem, which was played as we left terra firma, and the cheers which greeted our departure.

In a couple of minutes after leaving the Gardens, we were fairly over the Ormeau Road, not very far from the bridge and could see distinctly the crowds who thronged around. The wind at this time seemed rather inclined to carry us towards Belfast Lough and, as a precautionary measure, Mr. Coxwell got out his grapnel. In a few seconds, however, as we ascended, the wind changed and we were carried in almost a straight line from Ormeau to Shaw's Bridge, over the canal. We were now beginning thoroughly to get at home and the view that stretched out before us was magnificent.

Two loughs – Belfast and Strangford – were thoroughly in sight from end to end. We were on the look out for Lough Neagh and, suddenly, what had appeared to be the sun shining on a cloud burst forth to our view as Lough Neagh. This, in some respects, was the most enjoyable part of our trip. The magnificent view that we saw all around us — the fertile valley of the Lagan, with the silvery river glittering through it and the hamlets sleeping quietly in the evening sun — was a scene which cannot be forgotten.

The perfect stillness was, if possible, still more wonderful. We were still ascending rapidly and in a very short time, after remaining almost stationary, we passed through out first cloud. The effect of this was marvellous. As we ascended, it appeared as if we were passing through a white, fleecy kind of smoke, but still we could catch glimpses of the earth. A second or two more and we had fairly got above the cloud and could see far above us the clear unbroken sky and the sun shining brightly. The earth was entirely lost in its place and we had the clouds lying at our feet like snow.

A change in the wind seemed likely to drive us seaward once more and Mr. Coxwell deemed it prudent to attempt our descent. This was much more easily managed than we had at all anticipated. Our grapnel caught first in a tree, but did not take there; next it entwined itself in a hedge, but once more broke loose and, after leaving its mark in a field, we came safely to anchor in a grass field of a Mr. William Martin, of Lisdoonan, about three miles from Saintfield.

We had necessarily a few bumps in our descent, but, owing to the clear directions and admirable skill and coolness of Mr. Coxwell, none of the party received even a scratch. It was here that we saw the advantage of having the car made of an elastic material like basket-work. A more solid structure would have been broken to pieces. The country people were assembled in crowds and rendered their best assistance in getting the mammoth balloon safely ungassed and packed and sent off to Belfast, although they would light their pipes whilst the gas was escaping in all directions from the heaving monster.

The whole party returned by the last train to Belfast from Ballygowan. To those who have never undertaken a journey in a balloon we may say that the motion is not in the slightest degree unpleasant and it would indeed be more correct to say that it was quite imperceptible. The interest excited by this event was very great. Whenever we came in our journey near enough to distinguish objects, we could see crowds of people eagerly watching our movements. The entire time of our trip was, as nearly as possible, twenty-six minutes and the highest point which we reached was about a mile and a quarter from the earth.

Found among the annual reports of
The Belfast Botanic and Horticultural Society
July 8th, 1864

Thomas Drummond (1790–1835), a Scottish botanist and explorer, whose only official position was as the first curator of the Botanic Gardens in Belfast. He took up the role in 1828, after a two-year expedition of the Arctic regions of Canada under Captain John Franklin.

While in Belfast, he assembled 50 two-volume copies of his exsiccata of American mosses, entitled Musci Americani, which indulgence – coupled with accusations of severe alcoholism – led to tension with the management of the garden.

He left under a cloud in 1830 and almost immediately embarked on a botanisation of the southern United States, with no planned end date. Contracting cholera, he continued with his work, documenting hundreds of new plant and bird species, before heading to Havana.

In June of that year, his colleague Dr. William Hooker received three boxes from Cuba, containing no plants, but only Drummond's few possessions. Later, a letter arrived, dated March 11th, 1835, confirming Drummond's death. Conflicting reports suggest the botanist died of yellow fever, septicaemia, or falling into a bear pit and subsequent mauling.

Named for the mouth of the river, where the water meets the sand, Belfast is built on water, looking out to the sea. Millies were up to their ankles in it, shipbuilders could go up to their waists, and the city's drunks, its suicides and its misadventurers, went further than either, headfirst into Lough or Lagan and down. As the river flows into the Irish Sea, the sea washes in on the tide and Belfast, once a port town, gives to the world and it takes.

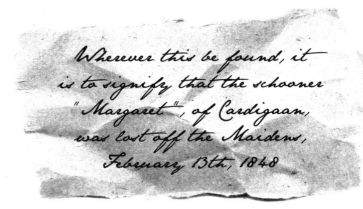

Wherever this be found, it is to signify that the schooner "Margaret", of Cardigaan, was lost off the Maidens, February 13th, 1848

Found in a bottle at Queen's Island
September 1849

SENSATIONAL AFFAIR AT WHITEHEAD
BELFAST GIRL FALLS OVER CLIFF
DROPS 160 FEET TO ROCKS BELOW
UNTOWARD ENDING TO PLAY

A sensational affair occurred on the famous Blackhead cliffs, near Whitehead, yesterday afternoon, when a Belfast girl, Lily Cooper (18), 22 Norwood Street, Belfast, fell to the rocks below, a distance of 160 feet, sustaining severe injuries.

The girl and her companion, Minnie Agnew, of 14 Norwood Street, had gone to Whitehead for the afternoon.

It appears that they met four youths and when playing with one of them on the cliff path, she fell.

The unfortunate girl resides with her widowed mother and she and her companion are both employed by Mr. R. M'Farland, fruiterer, 164 Sandy Row, Belfast.

——————————— ON AFTERNOON TRIP ———————————

The two girls met, it is stated, the four boys at Belfast Railway Station, with whom they travelled to Whitehead. There they separated, the two girls going round to Blackhead alone.

Later the boys joined them again on the path which leads to the lighthouse.

Lily Cooper and her companion had some sandwiches with them and as they intended returning to Whitehead for tea, they gave them to the boys.

Afterwards Lily Cooper commenced to gather primroses. One

of the boys, it appears, ran towards her and playfully wrestled with her for a piece of string, the girl falling over the cliff.

News of the terrible affair was conveyed to Chief Officer Ryan, Blackhead Lighthouse, who, accompanied by Lighthouse Keeper Kerron, rushed to the base of the cliff, taking with them an improvised stretcher.

A telephone message was sent to the police and for medical assistance, and Sergeant R.S. Smith and Dr. W. Martin, J.P., hurried to the scene.

——————————— SEVERE INTERNAL INJURIES ———————————
The girl was found in an unconscious condition. She was taken to the lighthouse, where it was found she was suffering from severe internal injuries.

Later she was conveyed to the Royal Victoria Hospital, Belfast, where she lies in a critical condition.

One of the youths, all of whom were panic-stricken at the untoward ending to their fun, has been detained by the Whitehead police, but as yet no charge has been preferred against him.

Northern Whig
April 25th, 1931

FOUND IN THE LAGAN

An inquest was held touching the death of Martha M'Cormick, a middle-aged woman. The body of the deceased was discovered between two logs in the River Lagan, near Albert Bridge, on the 15th, by a lad named Samuel M'Conville. The husband stated that his wife left 11 North Ann Street, where they lodged, on the 8th. He never saw her again alive. She was in the habit of absenting herself from home for long periods and occasionally took drink. The evidence of Dr Irvine showed that decomposition was so far advanced that he could not state the cause of death, but it was probably drowning. The skin had been eaten off the face evidently by rats. A verdict of "Found dead" was returned.*

Morning News
January 22nd, 1904

---

* The *Irish News* of 26 January 1904 reported that Martha M'Cormick returned alive the following Sunday.

ARE YOU A DIVINER?

The faculty of water-divination claimed by some favoured folk is now, I think, generally admitted. Time was, and that not so long ago, when water-diviners were universally regarded in much the same light as fortune-tellers with cards and such-like transparent charlatans. To-day even such responsible bodies as our sanitary boards commonly employ the water-diviner's services.

The modus operandi is quite simple. You cut off a leading branch of willow or sallow or, even better, of hazel and trim it and a branch into the figure of the letter Y. Grasp the arms of the letter with a certain torsion grip, the shank projecting forward, your thumbs upward, little fingers in advance. Walk slowly. When you pass over a spring the projecting shank "assumes the perpendicular", and, if you are an old hand, you can pronounce on the probable depth of the spring and its output from the vigour of the "pull". If you find no unusual sensation, even when passing over an obvious spring, then you may safely conclude that you are not a "water-medium". The writer has distinctly felt the downward-dip tendency of the hazel-shank when over a powerful spring, but cannot regard himself as a good water-diviner. Readers may like to try if they possess this beneficent power.

"O.", Ballyroney

Northern Whig
1931

THE SAILOR'S HORNPIPE
IN CAXTON STREET

Good people pay attention and listen to my song,
I'll sing to you a verse or two, I won't detain you long;
I came home from sea the other day, a fair lass I did meet.
She asked me to go along with her and dance in Jackson's Street.

"Jack, as you can't dance too well, will you then have a treat?
Will you have a glass of brandy or something you will take?
At nine o'clock this evening, I'll see you at the train;
And if ever you come this road, Jack, you will give us a call again."

When the dinner was over, the whiskey did come in;
Then round the floor with Maggie I danced the merry tune.
And the other couple they did dance
A double-shuffle all round the room.

When the supper was over I prepared and went to bed,
I shortly fell asleep, the truth, I do declare;
When I awakened in the morning nothing could I spy,
But a woman's shift and apron there at the foot of the bed did lie.

The daylight was past and the night was coming on,
I put on the shift and apron — to the quay I did run;
And when I got my foot aboard, the sailors they did say,
"By the word, Jack, you have caught the clock since you've been away!

"Is that the new Spring fashion they've got upon the shore?
Where is the shop they sell them — do you think there are any more?"
Says the Captain to me, "Jack, I thought you were Newry bound?
You might have got a better suit than that for less than three pounds."

"I met a girl in Heyberry Street, she asked me away to dance,
She stole away my heart with her roguish Irish glance;
She danced to my destruction — I suffered so complete.
I'll take my oath I'll go no more to dance in Jackson Street."

Come all you jolly seamen, a warning take by me,
Be sure to choose a comrade before you get on the spree,
Be sure and keep out of Jackson Street or you will rue the day
With a woman's shift and apron you will have to go to sea.

Anon.
(fl.1890–1918)

SHIPS SAILORS WON'T SAIL

There is nothing maritime-concerning about which sailors are
more superstitious than the naming of ships.

Even big firms like Messrs Harland and Wolff, the builders
of the illustrious White Star line, are not quite exempt from this

weakness. The Oceanic, that splendid new liner of which we have lately heard so much, was named after a "lucky ship", the original Oceanic having been the pioneer of the long, narrow liners with which the White Stars set the fashion to the world. She was always a fortunate vessel, making good times and avoiding disasters and, if there is luck in any name, the modern leviathan certainly could not have been more wisely christened. It is worth noting, by the way, that the second Oceanic, after her launch and partial fitting, steamed out of dock on a Thursday night and was kept lying in Belfast Lough until Saturday, rather than let her proceed on what was actually her first trip (a mile or two down the Lough) on a Friday.

A very amusing incident illustrative of these same superstitions took place off the well-known "Twin Islands", on which the White Stars are built, some years ago. A gentleman employed by the company, wishing to give the workmen a useful lesson as to the folly of superstitions about names, had a small boat built for himself, and christened her The Hearse. Every man on the islands predicted her speedy destruction and a large and lugubrious crowd collected to see her start for her maiden trip, manned by her owner alone. She had not gone a couple of hundred years down the channel before she struck on an islet and went to pieces! Her owner swam ashore with some difficulty and that was the end of the lesson.

Another large and famous Belfast shipbuilding firm, consisting of two partners, were the builders of the two luckless Lord Dufferins. One was built for a line trading from Belfast. After a few voyages, she disappeared and neither she nor her crew were ever heard of again. The second Lord Dufferin, built for a Liverpool line, was lost with all hands on her maiden trip, about a year later.

The history of the Daphne, built on the Clyde about the beginning of the eighties, is one of extraordinary disaster. She commenced her sea life by capsizing at her launch and drowning a hundred and fifty people. This was sufficient to stamp her as a "wrong 'un" in the eyes of every seaman and she proceeded to justify the character she had earned by ripping herself upon the anchors of another vessel in the little harbour of Portrush, Co. Antrim, whither she had run upon when short of coal on one other early voyage. She was raised with some trouble, fitted out afresh, re-christened Rosa, and sent off again. Not long afterwards, she sank again off Larne, Belfast Lough. As no British crew could be obtained to work her and even owners were shy of such a record, a Greek trading company bought her, gave her a foreign name, and set to work in the Mediterranean, since when her career, whatever it may have been, has been buried in silence.

Lisburn Standard
May 1917

PASSION FOR THE SEA
YOUNG BELFAST GIRL
WORK ON THE WIND-JAMMER
VOYAGE TO AUSTRALIA

A passion for the sea is so strong in Nancie M. Moore, a 17-year-old Belfast girl, that she has crossed the world in a four-masted barque as an ordinary seaman and prefers that mode of travelling to any other. At the age of 16, she urged her parents to allow her to make a voyage as a passenger in the four-masted barque L'Avenir from Glasgow to Mariehamn.

"I had made arrangements before my parents knew, but had to use a lot of argument and persuasion before they would give me permission to go. They thought one voyage would be enough for me, but it only made me still more enthusiastic," said Miss Moore.

SEAMAN'S DISCHARGE!

Proudly, yet shyly, Miss Moore showed the interviewer the discharge she received from the skipper upon her leaving the vessel at Port Lincoln, South Australia. She said she was going to frame the document when she returns to Belfast. She also treasures a two-shilling piece which the captain gave her in payment of wages earned on the 90-day voyage — a few cents more than she had earned, indeed, because of the exchange ratio. Her wages were expected to be 10 marks a month.

```
"S.V. Ponape,
Gustav Erikson,
Mariehamn.
```

```
This is to certify that Nancie M. Moore has served on board
the Finnish four-masted barque Ponape, gross register 2342
tons, as ordinary seaman during a voyage from Copenhagen
```

to Port Lincoln, South Australia, from October 20th 1934,
until January 18th, 1935; total time served 90 days. During
her stay on board, she has always acted in a sober and
good manner and done her duties to my entire satisfaction.
She is leaving the ship at her own request. Port Lincoln,
January 19th, 1935.

Carl Granith,
Master of the Ponape.

———————— *VOYAGE DESCRIBED* ————————

"On the last voyage, we left Copenhagen on October 21st and
proceeded north of the Shetland Islands because of the weather.
The usual route is north of the Orkney Isles. The sailing ships do
not go through the English Channel because, against head winds,
they cannot beat there; there is no room and at night or in fog it
might be dangerous. A good run was had and the line was reached in
33 days. We had been held up at the Canary Islands for a while and
also at Tristan Da Cunha, because of calm or very light winds. At
Tristan Da Cunha, we put in and four boats full of natives came out
to barter all kinds of things.

"An English parson came out and asked me to go ashore. I went
with a bodyguard at the risk of being marooned, if any wind came
before I could get on board. I spent five hours there looking over
the island.

"Then came Christmas Day, when we were about the latitude
of the Cape in 45. Next day, a sudden squall got up in the night,
followed by a gale and tore out all our sails except three. The wind
blew them to ribbons.

"A lovely wind took us across the Bight to Spencer Gulf, where
we were held up for four days beating up and down the coast. We
got into Port Lincoln after 88 days from Copenhagen. I went by
steamer to Adelaide, where I spent three days and then went by train
to Melbourne and Sydney."

Miss Moore will be in Wellington till she receives a cable from the
skipper of the Ponape. A wheat cargo is being sought by the skipper
and it takes five or six weeks to load a cargo of wheat. Miss Moore will
then return home on board the Ponape.

Evening Post, Wellington
March 6th, 1935

THE RISKS OF WALKING ABOUT
SOME PERILS OF FOOT PASSENGERS

On landing at Belfast, a poor fellow, evidently feeling ill, leaned against some railings.

As he remained in that attitude for a long time, someone went to his help. Then it was found that the stranger's head had slipped down between two spikes and that he, being unable to extricate himself or even to shout for help, had been strangled. He was quite dead.

Guardian, London
April 15th, 1907

—— HUGE SHIP RUNS AMOK ——
LAUNCHES ITSELF BEFORE SCHEDULE
AMAZING SCENE AT BELFAST
THOUSANDS OF PEOPLE ESCAPE MIRACULOUSLY

One woman was killed and 15 other persons were injured, while hundreds of workmen and thousands of spectators had a miraculous escape from death, when the 23,000-ton aircraft-carrier, Formidable, launched itself at Belfast half an hour before schedule.

The crowd was horror-stricken as, with a terrific rending of metal and wood, the ship tore her way from the cradle and began to career down the slips entirely unsupported.

As huge pieces of the cradle were flung in all directions, spectators massed on each side of the slipway were in imminent danger. They would have been crushed to death had the ship overturned, but, by one chance in a million, it remained on an even keel as it gathered speed and plunged into the water amid dead silence from the petrified crowd.

Recorder, Australia
August 18th, 1939

COLLISION ON BELFAST LOUGH

A steamer collided with and overthrew a small lighthouse in Belfast Lough – the inmates being drowned.

Thames Examiner, London
November 19th 1892

PREMONITIONS OF THE SINKING OF THE TITANIC

1874 The poem, 'A Tryst' by American poet Celia Thaxter (d.1894), in which an iceberg and a liner finally make their destined rendezvous in the middle of the Atlantic. In Thaxter's poem, "They perished, every one".

1894 The novella *Futility, or The Wreck of the Titan* by Morgan Robertson, American short story writer. Robertson died of a heart attack, in poverty, three years after the tragedy.

1899 The novel *The Lost Liner* by Robert Cromie, Belfast-based science fiction author. The book has been out of print since 1899.

1908 Anton Johansson, a Scandinavian mystic, predicted the name of the sinking ship and named John Jacob Astor IV as a fatality. These predictions earned him notoriety.

1909–10 In 1910, W.T. Stead, American spiritualist, journalist, and activist, had a visionary dream of his own drowning. The following year, he had a consultation with Irish palmist, Chiero, who warned him to avoid travelling until after April 1912. Stead made the journey regardless and, during the disaster, helped women and children into the lifeboats and gave up his lifejacket to another passenger. His body was never recovered.

1912 William Ronald Brailey, prominent English Trance Clairvoyant and Psychometrist had a dream, warning him not to let his son take work aboard the Titanic. Theodore Ronald Brailey continued to play piano with the band as the ship sank.

January 1912 Edith Russell, American fashion journalist. During a trip to Africa, an Arab told her "Madame will have a very grave accident at sea." She made the voyage anyway and, in a letter to a friend, posted on April 10th, 1912 in Queenstown, she wrote, "I cannot get over my feeling of depression and premonition of trouble. How I wish it were over. I had a presentiment. Then the night before we sailed, I went to a fortune-teller who said I would lose every bit of jewellery, every one of my possessions, even my voice. 'Don't take the boat you are planning to take,' I was told. And the next day when we got alongside the ship I said to someone, 'I don't want to go'." Russell was rescued from the water and lived to the age of 96.

March 1912 J. Conan Middleton, English businessman, had a dream of astral-flying over the disaster. He cancelled his ticket.

The deaths of Theo Brailey and W.T. Stead on the Titanic would do more for Spiritualists in the spirit than in the flesh.

International Congress of Spiritualists
July 1912

THE WRECK OF THE TITAN

Amid the roar of escaping steam, and the bee-like buzzing of nearly three thousand human voices, raised in agonized screams and callings from within the inclosing walls, and the whistling of air through hundreds of open dead-lights as the water, entering the holes of the crushed and riven starboard side, expelled it, the Titan moved slowly backward and launched herself into the sea, where she floated low on her side — a dying monster, groaning with her death-wound.

Morgan Robertson
1898

A COMPARISON OF WHITE STAR'S TITANIC AND MORGAN ROBERTSON'S TITAN

	TITANIC	TITAN
Flag of registry	British	British
Month of Travel	April	April
Propellers	3	3
Side of ship damaged by iceberg	Starboard	Starboard
Passenger and crew capacity	3,000	3,000
Passengers and crew aboard	2,201	2,000
Displacement	52,310 tons	70,000 tons
Length	882.9 ft	800 ft
Available Lifeboats	20	24
Watertight Bulkheads	15	19
Top speed	22 knots	24–25 knots
Engines	Triple Expansion and Turbine	Triple

Astrological conditions on the night April 14th/15th, 1912
*Moon in Aquarius; Mercury in Aries, in retrograde .** *

A BIBLIOGRAPHY OF SPECULATIVE FICTION WRITTEN BY AUTHORS LOST ON THE TITANIC

John Jacob Astor IV (1864–1912): *A Journey in Other Worlds: A Romance of the Future* (1894)

Jacques Futrelle (1875–1912): *The Thinking Machine* (1907), *The Diamond Master* (1909), *The Flying Eye* (1912)

F.D. Millet (1846–1912): *Capillary Crime and Other Stories* (1892)

W.T. Stead (1849–1912): *If Christ Came to Chicago* (1894), *Blastus, the King's Chamberlain: A Political Romance* (1898), *The Despised Sex* (1903).

THE STORM
Detention of cross-channel steamers

Last night Belfast was visited with a storm of unusual violence. From about eleven o'clock the wind blew with great force, and towards one o'clock this morning it freshened into a perfect hurricane, sweeping chimney-pots and slates off the roofs and carrying them about in all directions, while in many streets signboards and projecting lamps were blown away. In Corporation Street several chimneys were torn down, carrying portions of the roofing with them, and the occupants of the houses got so alarmed that they were propped to prevent them from falling. A house in Ballymacarrett, where a penny show has been held for some time, came down with a great crash about three o'clock this morning. The lately erected boat-house, beside the Central Railway Bridge, on the banks of the Lagan, was blown down, and a large portion of the timber swept into the sea. A telegraph pole at the Queen's Bridge appeared to be falling, and a party of linesmen were immediately at work to secure it. The new Methodist

---

* Within astrology, the planet Mercury controls communication, both verbal and non-verbal. In the public sphere, it is believed to influence mass-communication, transportation, commerce, and technology. When Mercury is in retrograde, its influence becomes purely negative.

Church which is in course of erection at Carlisle Circus was slightly injured, having had a large piece of masonry blown off the top of the building. In the outskirts of the town much damage to house property is done. Several small trees have been uprooted, and fences and palings have been injured severely. The Fleetwood steamer, Thomas Dugdale, arrived at eight o'clock, having experienced most severe weather during the passage. The Dublin steamer, Iron Duke, which left Dublin at nine o'clock last night arrived here shortly after eleven o'clock after a passage of unprecedented severity. The Liverpool and Barrow steamers have not yet come into port, and their arrival is being anxiously waited for by a large crowd of people on the quay.

The tug-steamer Alderman Ridley reports lying at Bangor Pier till about one o'clock this morning. She was then forced to leave for fear of being dashed to pieces by the violence of the storm. She went out and cast anchor a short distance from the wall. The anchor chain broke when she had to steam to Belfast, which, from the violence of the gale, she was scarcely able to reach. When passing the Twin Islands, one of the river lighthouses on the South Island was blown away. The tug reached the quay in safety at about four o'clock.

Ulster Echo
January 7th, 1839

THE FOG
BELFAST WRAPPED IN MIST

The fog fiend, which has held England in its grip for the past two days, reached Belfast to-day and, from an early hour the city was wrapped in a thick mist. Business was carried on with the aid of gas and electricity right up till the afternoon and, though the fog was thick, it was not sufficiently dense to interfere much with the street traffic in the principal thoroughfares. In the vicinity of the docks, there was some dislocation of traffic, apart from the non-arrival of some of the cross-Channel steamers, and it was impossible to see many yards down the river.

Belfast News-Letter
April 13th, 1832

Some things lost in the fog of 1832: Asian cholera; maps; ships; Babbage's Difference Engine; cholera preventive costume; water-testing kit; gentleman's umbrella; gold watch; lamp; hook; line; sinker.

THE FOG IN BELFAST
LAMENTABLE OCCURRENCE AT THE DOCKS
MAN AND HORSE DROWNED

The fog again descended on the city this morning and caused considerable inconvenience to traffic. It was not so bad as yesterday and the cross-Channel steamers arrived at their berths in good time. A sad fatality, as the result of yesterday afternoon's fog, was brought to light this morning, at about six o'clock, when the body of a man named Thomas Tinsley was found in the water near the North Twin Island. Tinsley was a driver in the employment of the Provincial Mineral Water Company, Bain's Place, and it appears that yesterday afternoon, at 2.45, he went to the Twins with a load of rubbish in his van for depositing at a place known as the Pithead, contiguous to Workman, Clark, & Co.'s North Yard. He had been there earlier in the day with a similar load, but after he had left in the afternoon nothing was heard of him till to-day when his body was found in the water beside his horse and van. The horse was also dead.

The van was empty and it was obvious that the unfortunate man had driven into the water in the fog. It is probable that when he was returning to the city he took a wrong turn, the fog being especially dense at this place yesterday afternoon.

The police at York Road Barracks were informed and Constable Andrew Douglas had the remains conveyed to the Morgue, pending an inquest. The deceased was about 45 years of age and resided at 13 Cape Street, Falls Road.

Belfast Evening Telegraph
February 11th, 1904

Some things lost in the fog of 1904: Man; horse.

*T*o collect the disparate parts of this strange city is to rationalise them, but they cannot be rationalised: for, the more they are moved around, the less they agree to fit. The project of collecting and categorising the odd can never be completed, because, if these things could be categorised or collected, they would not be of so much interest.

This book gives only the outline of the shadow.

ACKNOWLEDGEMENTS

Eternal thanks to Aislínn, my beloved, for her frequent bouts of patience and her first-rate second opinion; to Liam O'Reilly at PRONI, who knew where I should be looking before I knew what I was looking for; to the staff at Belfast Central Library; to the unerringly helpful Catherine Hatt of the McClay Library; to the air-conditioning of that same institution; to Michelle, and everyone at Blackstaff, who removed only the right things; to all the rights-givers; and, of course, to my parents, without whom I wouldn't be possible.

The editor and publisher gratefully acknowledge permission to include the following copyright material:

CALVERT, RAYMOND, 'The Ballad of William Bloat', reproduced by kind permission of Susan Calvert.

GREGORY, PADRAIC, 'The Late Reader' and 'The Ghost' from *Padraic Gregory: Complete Ballads* (Lagan Press, 2013); and 'The Stranger-Mite's Clothes', all reproduced by kind permission of Patrick Gregory. www.padraicgregory.com

Chapter opener images:
'Nora's Grave', from *Belfast Evening Telegraph*
'The Botanic Gardens', Shutterstock, Morphart Creation
'The Goligher Circle', from W.J. Crawford, *Hints and observations for those investigating the phenomena of spiritualism* (1918)
'The Naked Turk', from *Irish News*
'The Ripper in Belfast', from *Illustrated Police News*

ABOUT THE AUTHOR

Reggie Chamberlain-King quickly sped past youth and education into decrepit early adulthood, becoming, by cold hard luck, a writer, musician, and broadcaster. He makes frequent appearances on Radio Ulster's *Arts Extra* and was, for four years, the cultural attaché on *After Midnight* with Stuart Bailie.

He has written several plays, including *The Ballad of Lilliburlero* for BBC NI Events, and *The Down Chorus*, for Wireless Mystery Theatre. His work has appeared on BBC Radio 3 and BBC Radio 4 and has been broadcast in Germany, Canada and the United States.

He is a co-founder, actor, musician and continuity announcer with Wireless Mystery Theatre and author of the cult mystery series *The Brittaine & Molloy Inquiry Quarterly*. *Weird Belfast* is his first book.

For more on Reggie Chamberlain-King visit www.thestuffedowl.co.uk
Or follow him on Twitter @Reggie_C_King